Good Afternoon,

Ladies and Gentlemen!

BORIS GOLDOVSKY

Good Afternoon, Ladies and Gentlemen!

Intermission Scripts from the Met Broadcasts

INDIANA UNIVERSITY PRESS

Bloomington

Library of Congress Cataloging in Publication Data

Goldovsky, Boris.
     Good afternoon, ladies and gentlemen!

        1. Opera—Addresses, essays, lectures.   I. Title.
ML1700.G739   1984   782.1   83-49338
ISBN 0-253-32588-9
ISBN 0-253-32587-0 companion cassette
1   2   3   4   5   88   87   86   85   84

Contents

Preface

It was almost forty years ago that I was first asked to preside over "Opera News on the Air," the first-intermission feature of the radio broadcasts of the Metropolitan Opera in New York City. My initial greeting, "Good afternoon, ladies and gentlemen," soon became a sort of trademark of which I was quite fond. At some point, however (it was in the 1960s, I believe), someone in authority decided that calling the radio audience "ladies and gentlemen" was a bit too pompous and that my opening words should be less formal. I suggested that I might simply thank the gentleman who had introduced me; so I changed to, "Thank you, Milton Cross," and later to, "Thank you, Peter Allen." I am thankful for their gracious introductions, but I am even more grateful to them for relieving me of the necessity of relating the story of the opera. Knowing that the regular announcer will supply a detailed synopsis of the plot has allowed me to concentrate on some special aspect of the opera of the day, an approach that eventually became known as "musical and dramatic analysis." In the same way, the scripts included here assume that the reader knows the plots of the operas, though for a few of the less familiar ones, I have added short plot summaries.

In my Saturday afternoon broadcasts, I have always illustrated my talk with musical excerpts, relying on my pianistic abilities to make the analysis more meaningful. The simplest of these musical examples are printed in the text, but for readers who wish to hear the more elaborate ones, I have prepared a cassette containing over 250 of my piano illustrations.

The content of these scripts varies greatly, reflecting aspects of opera that I personally find fascinating. Texaco, which has sponsored the broadcasts since 1940, and those directly in charge of the intermission features (Henry and Geraldine Souvaine and, more recently, Richard Mohr) have always given me a free hand in the selection of the "theme" of each script and have often come forth with valuable suggestions. At first, there was a bit of nervousness. It was estimated that during each broadcast, approximately seven million listeners tuned in at one time or another, and it was considered unwise to antagonize them by complicated and excessively erudite discussions. And since I lived in Boston, where I taught opera and headed my own professional opera company, I was repeatedly warned not to use any technical terms (such as *tonic, dominant,* or—Lord forbid—*subdominant!*) and quite particularly to keep in mind that I was not "lecturing at Harvard"! All these strictures disappeared in time, and as the reader of the present volume will discover, no topic is on the blacklist and no holds are barred.

I want to thank Texaco Inc. for permission to use the scripts and the musical illustrations and Eleanor Eisenmenger for her invaluable help in preparing the cassette and the printed illustrations.

Good Afternoon,
Ladies and Gentlemen!

AÏDA

by Giuseppe Verdi

Broadcast December 16, 1978

Cassette illustrations 1—9

Every OPERA LOVER knows that *Aïda* is a foremost example of "Grand Opera." It has gigantic and spectacular scenery, displayed in no fewer than seven magnificent settings. It calls for eight outstanding solo singers and surrounds them with hundreds of choristers, dancers, and supernumeraries, most of whom are dressed in exotic and expensive costumes. It requires a very large orchestra, which is augmented by stage bands and various other instruments playing onstage and backstage. It is truly grand! And yet there is another, no less impressive side to the opera: it also presents an artful display of subtle psychological nuances occurring in episodes of great intimacy.

Most of the important dramatic business of the opera is transacted with only two singers onstage, during five long duets involving Aïda, Amneris, Radames, and Amonasro. And surprisingly often the action is accompanied by a drastically reduced and very subdued orchestral ensemble. The fact is that in no other of Giuseppe Verdi's 27 operas is there so much soft playing by such small groups of orchestral instruments. The opening of the orchestral Prelude is introduced by just half of the first violins; they are soon joined by the other half, all of them muted and playing pianissimo [1].* Later, when the curtain rises on the second scene of the first act, on the Temple of Vulcan, Verdi employs even more limited instrumental means. During the initial 52 measures of this scene, the or-

---

*Throughout this book, the numbers in square brackets refer to musical examples on the companion tape.

chestra in the pit does not play a single note. The only sounds are those of offstage harps accompanying the voices of the high priestess and her assistants. When the orchestra resumes its playing, the enchanting dance tune is presented by only three flutes supported by pizzicato strings [2].

There are countless other passages in *Aïda* when the orchestral accompaniment is entrusted to just a handful of instruments, producing an effect more appropriate to a piece of chamber music than to an opera, not to mention grand opera. This has puzzled me for a long time, until I realized that these intimate and quiet beginnings and interludes provide a stunning contrast to the towering passions that erupt in the course of each scene. For the essence of the opera lies not in its surface trappings or in the number of its participants, but in the overwhelming and truly volcanic passions of its protagonists. Isaac Bashevis Singer, the Nobel Prize winner, once remarked that "God was very frugal in bestowing gifts on human beings. God didn't give us enough intellect, or enough physical strength. But when it came to emotions and passions, God was very lavish. He gave us so many emotions and such strong ones that every human being is a millionaire in emotions!" If that is true of ordinary people, then Amneris, Amonasro, Aïda, and Radames must surely be classified as multimillionaires or even billionaires.

Each of the seven scenes of Aïda begins in a subdued tone, but it does not take long until the various protagonists start spending their rich reserves of passionate feelings. At first they may appear cool and controlled, but it takes only a spark to start a conflagration. In the opening scene, the initial conversation between Amneris and Radames seems quite harmless and almost trifling [3], but a few measures later a momentary embarrassment on the part of Radames and one careless loving glance he directs at Aïda suffices to ignite Amneris's suspicions and to arouse intense fear in Radames that he may have betrayed his secret. Now the calm musical and emotional surface is rent asunder by the flames of jealousy and fear [4]. When Aïda begins to express the woes of her heart caused by the rumors of war, as well as by her hopeless amorous infatuation, Verdi creates one of his marvelous ensembles, in which the voices of several participants—each expressing his own private passionate concern—blend in exciting, harmonious entity [5].

Sometimes these seesawing alternations between quiet episodes and emotional explosions, between whispers and shouting, are carried on for an entire section of the opera. For example, in the first scene of the second act, Princess Amneris displays her devilishly clever inquisitorial genius by gradually tricking Aïda into revealing her secret love affair. I doubt whether Verdi or his librettist, Ghislanzoni, had ever heard of a lie detector; and yet the technique employed by Amneris is essentially the same as that used by the operators of the modern polygraph. Amneris first puts her lovely slave at ease by assuring her that her troubles will soon be over and that happiness is in store for her. Then, little by little, Amneris starts using key words to see what effect they have. "Time will cure your unhappiness," she says, "and so will *love*." Amneris is by no means certain that Aïda suffers from amorous pangs, but her very first test word elicits a significant effect. For as soon as Aïda hears the word *amore* ("love"), her face turns pale, and, trembling with excitement, she repeats: "Amore, amore! gaudio tormento, soave ebbrezza, ansia crudel!" ("Love, love, joy and torment, delicious rapture, cruel anxiety!") [6].

Now Amneris is more determined than ever to discover the truth. She is going to weaken Aïda's defenses, lull whatever suspicions Aïda may have, and make her betray the name of her secret admirer. "Trust to my love," Amneris says, "confide in me. Was it perhaps one of our soldier boys who poured this sweet anguish into your heart?" The orchestral passage that accompanies this "sweet anguish" sentence is entrusted to just three instruments: two clarinets and a bassoon. This phrase exudes such cajoling sweetness that one can almost feel the gentle sisterly caress—a pinch on the cheek or a chucking under the chin—by means of which Amneris seeks to assure Aïda of her friendship and good will. Now comes the key sentence. "Not everyone is necessarily unlucky in war," Amneris tells Aïda, enunciating her words casually without putting too much emphasis on them. "Just because our valiant leader was mortally wounded on the field of battle. . . ." Amneris is not even able to finish the sentence, for Aïda's reaction is immediate and convulsive: "What are you saying? Heaven help me!" Aïda's vocal line, as well as its accompaniment, now erupts in a sudden exclamatory rush:

Che mai di - ce - sti!   mi - se-ra!

Amneris pretends to be surprised by the violence of Aïda's reaction. "Yes," she adds, while the orchestral strings murmur in a subdued whisper, "Yes, Radames was slain by your people."

These words lead to another burst of unhappiness on the part of Aïda. But in contrast to Aïda's eruptions, Amneris remains outwardly, as well as vocally and orchestrally, calm. "Why should you weep?" she asks. "The gods have avenged the defeat of your people." But Aïda is inconsolable. "No," she exclaims, "the gods have always been against me!" Now it is Amneris's turn to lose her temper. "Tremble!" she bursts out angrily. "I have read your heart! You love him!" And now comes the clincher, which Amneris softly hisses at Aïda over a pianissimo accompaniment of orchestral strings. "Look at my face! I deceived you—Radames is alive!"

Quite beside herself, Aïda falls on her knees shouting: "Alive! Ah, the gods be thanked!"

Aïda can no longer deny that she loves Radames, but there is still another emotional shock in store for her. Against the barely audible throbbing of cellos and double basses and supported only by two soft clarinets, Amneris, without raising her voice, delivers the coup de grâce: "You love him!" she tells Aïda. "But so do I—you understand? I am your rival, I, the daughter of the pharaohs." Provoked beyond endurance by Amneris's arrogance, Aïda is about to expose her secret and proclaim that she also is the daughter of a king, but aware of the disastrous consequences of such a revelation, she catches herself in time and collapses at Amneris's feet, pleading for mercy. "Have pity on my grief. You are happy and powerful. I live only for this immense love!" And here again Verdi reverts to the chamber music style of instrumental accompaniment. Aïda's eloquent lament is supported at first by just a flute and a bassoon, then joined in the second measure by another flute and a single clarinet [7].

But it is in vain that Aïda begs for pity or mercy. From here on Amneris has nothing but hatred for her *abborrita rivale* (her "detested rival").

For if Aïda calls her love immense, Amneris's feelings for Radames are no less towering. Amneris describes them without reservation, in the first scene of the last act, while standing face to face with Radames. He, it so happens, has not a scintilla of sympathy for Amneris, and now that he has lost Aïda, he is looking only for death. But Amneris cannot bear the thought that Radames will be condemned to die. "No," she exclaims, "you must live, live for me, for my love! For your sake I have suffered mortal anguish. I lay awake nights weeping. My fatherland, my throne, my life—all, all, I am ready to sacrifice for you!" [8].

We know that Verdi was always looking for violent, colorful situations. It is clear that in *Aïda* he was granted a full share of them. As the great French opera composer Georges Bizet remarked in a letter, "As a musician, I tell you that if you were to suppress hatred, adultery, fanaticism, or evil, it would no longer be possible to write a single note of music." And yet music has another function not mentioned in Bizet's letter, one exemplified in *Aïda*. It is best described in Thomas Mann's *Magic Mountain*, a novel that otherwise has very little to do with music. The hero, Hans Castorp, spends several years in a Swiss sanatorium for consumptives, where, among other experiences, he witnesses the death of his cousin. Toward the end of the book, he gets interested in listening to phonograph records. One that has a special bearing on his own personal problems, is a recording of the last scene of *Aïda*. Long before I had any interest in anything related to opera, this particular episode in the *Magic Mountain* fascinated me and gave me an insight into the very special power of music: to transform reality, to make us forget what is ugly and sordid and become aware of what is heavenly and sublime. Here is the way Thomas Mann describes the final episode of the opera: The scene takes place in the lower level of the temple, in the underground tomb, while over the heads of the two lovers the priests murmur their prayers and spread their hands in ritualistic gestures.

> "Tu—in questa tomba?" ["You, in this tomb?"] comes the inexpressibly moving, sweet and at the same time heroic voice of Radames, in mingled horror and rapture. Yes, she has found her way to him, the beloved one for whose sake he has forfeited life and honor, she has awaited him here, to die with him; and the exchange of song between the two . . . pierced the soul of our solitary night-watcher to its very depth. . . . But he would have been less ravished by the sounds, had not the situation which gave them

birth prepared his spirit to yield to the sweetness of the music. It was *so* beautiful, that Aïda should have found her way to the condemned Radames, to share his fate forever! The condemned one protested, quite properly, against the sacrifice of the precious life; but in his tender, despairing "No, no, troppo sei bella" ["You are too lovely"] was the intoxication of final union with her whom he had thought never to see again. It needed no effort of imagination to enable Hans Castorp to feel with Radames all this intoxication, all this gratitude. . . . What was it, considered with the eye of reason, that was happening here? Two human beings buried alive, . . . would here together—or, more horrible still, one after the other—succumb to the pangs of hunger, and thereafter the process of putrefaction would do its unspeakable work, until two skeletons remained, each totally indifferent and insensible to the other's presence or absence. This was the real, objective fact . . . , which was triumphantly put in the shade by the music and the beauty of the theme. . . . Their voices rose *unisono* to the blissful sustained note leading into the octave, as they assured each other that heaven was opening, and the light of its eternity [was] streaming forth before their yearning eyes. [9]

ARABELLA

by Richard Strauss

Broadcast March 5, 1983   Cassette illustrations 10–18

MANY OPERA LOVERS are puzzled and somewhat troubled when male roles are sung by women wearing male clothing. Almost everyone readily accepts these "trouser roles" when the characters are children: the shepherd boy in *Tannhäuser*, Gretel's little brother, Hänsel, Boris Godunov's son, Feodor, little Yniold in *Pelléas and Mélisande*, or the title role in Ravel's *L'Enfant et les sortilèges*.

But when these vocally female and dramatically male characters are older, and especially when they are involved in love affairs with women, many opera fans find the theatrical situations less than believable. "Doesn't Ilia in *Idomeneo* realize," they ask, "that Idamante—the man with whom she is so much in love—is 'really' a girl? And what about Sophie in *Der Rosenkavalier*? Isn't she aware that her beloved Octavian is in reality a woman? And when the plot demands that a woman—for whatever good reason—masquerade as a man, how is it credible that the other characters onstage do not catch on that the person wearing trousers—be she Fidelio, or Despina in *Così fan tutte*, or Zdenka in *Arabella*—is really a girl dressed as a man?"

In answering these seemingly rational and legitimate questions, it is useful to keep in mind that there are two very important groups of people who find this sort of thing not only credible but actually very advantageous. I am referring to singers and composers of opera. Contraltos and sopranos are very fond of roles where they have a chance to impersonate male characters. It enables them to develop new and different acting skills: to learn to wear men's clothing and to indulge in vigorous, authoritative ways of walking and gesturing. In her memoirs, Lotte Lehmann confesses that when she was chosen to sing the title role in Richard Strauss's _Ariadne auf Naxos_, she was greatly saddened at no longer being able to portray that opera's young male composer. Of course, there is nothing new or surprising in this hankering to impersonate men. The idiosyncrasies of male and female behavior have always been a favorite topic of stage presentations. The current successes of such films as _Victor–Victoria_ and _Tootsie_ are only the most recent manifestations of this trend.

Famous actresses and opera singers have not been content to limit themselves to the officially sanctioned trouser roles. Sarah Bernhardt insisted on impersonating Hamlet. Maria Malibran—one of the most celebrated operatic superstars of the first half of the nineteenth century—was a greatly acclaimed Desdemona in Rossini's _Otello_. But she was also very fond of occasionally singing the role of Otello in the same opera. This sex change was not always a success, at least not visually. Frederic Chopin saw Malibran's Otello in Paris 150 years ago, when the role of Desdemona was sung by the equally renowned Schröder-Devrient. "Malibran is small," Chopin wrote to a friend, "while the German lady is huge; and it really looked as if Desdemona would strangle Otello!"

This Schröder-Devrient, by the way, was herself very fond of singing "trouser roles," and she also would occasionally sing Otello in Rossini's opera. She was famous for her impersonation of Fidelio, and Richard Wagner was only too delighted to have her sing and act the trouser role of Adriano in _Rienzi_. These thefts of tenor roles by female singers were by no means exceptional, nor were they abandoned later on. Some 25 years after Malibran trod the boards made up as an African Moor, her younger sister, Pauline Viardot, made a sensation by putting on a Greek chiton and a chlamys (Greeks did not wear trousers) and impersonating Gluck's Orfeo. In our own century, Mary Garden fell in love with the title role of Massenet's _Le Jongleur de Notre Dame_ (which was written for a tenor) and had such success singing and acting the Juggler that even the composer had to admit that it was a good idea.

Particularly challenging, from the acting point of view, are roles— such as Octavian in Strauss's _Der Rosenkavalier_ or Zdenka in _Arabella_— that call for alternating masculine and feminine behavior. Think of Octavian, who starts out as a dashing cavalier, then becomes a shy and simpering chambermaid, but recovers his masculine appearance by the end of the first act. He is a man in the second act, where he must be able to manipulate a sword and hold a bunch of attacking hoodlums at bay. In the third act he starts out, ostensibly, as the naïve chambermaid and finally resumes his manly shape at the end of the opera. Zdenka must be similarly versatile. She must sound curt and boyish when talking with Matteo or worrying about his frenzied infatuation with Arabella [10]. A while later she displays an entirely different attitude and tone of voice when she is alone with her sister [11]. She is a boy throughout the second act and a thoroughly girlish girl in the last act. No wonder that singers are fond of such opportunities to show off their acting skills!

An even more important aspect of the trouser-role problem is found in the attitude of composers. As far as I can tell, all creators of opera, without exception, considered it perfectly normal that vocal sounds in the soprano range should issue from the lips of characters who—in the spoken theater—would have been acted by men. Mozart did not object to the male sopranos of his time singing Idamante in *Idomeneo* or Sextus in *La Clemenza di Tito*. Mozart's adolescent Cherubino—composed for a woman and always sung by a woman—is the granddaddy of many camouflaged page boys: Verdi's Oscar in *The Masked Ball*, his Tebaldo in *Don Carlo*, and Gounod's Stephano in *Romeo and Juliet*; as well as such adolescents as Siebel in *Faust*, Nicklausse in *The Tales of Hoffmann*, and Prince Orlofsky in *Die Fledermaus*. But trouser roles are not restricted to children, page boys and teenagers. Rossini quite regularly composed important male roles for contraltos. There are at least seven Rossini trouser roles among his lesser-known works, such as *Tancredi* and *Semiramide*. In the Met's production of Rossini's *The Siege of Corinth*, Shirley Verrett took the male role of Cleontes.

All this may seem a bit perplexing and unrealistic, but the ultimate justification of trouser roles is rooted in the very nature of opera. Singing with instrumental accompaniment is not a realistic concept to begin with. But it so happens that without it, opera simply would not exist. We might as well face the fact that vocal sounds in the soprano range do not necessarily have a gender. They are simply an extension of the basic artificiality of substituting singing for speech. Composers have accepted this special amplification of the singing syndrome without any qualms. Richard Strauss relished every opportunity to exercise his matchless gift for orchestral tone-painting, especially as it applied to roles that featured both masculine and feminine behavior. For instance, Octavian can be a virile man:

or a cute chambermaid [12].

In *Arabella* the musical transformations of Zdenka's personality are particularly fascinating. Because of the unusual complexity of her role, Strauss endows Zdenka with a great variety of descriptive and explanatory musical themes. Near the very beginning of the opera, Zdenka's mother explains the reason for the disguise. "He is really a girl," she says, pointing to the trouser-wearing Zdenka. "As a child she was a wild tomboy, and so we let her go around as a boy. We are not rich enough to bring out two girls in this town in keeping with our position." The mother's vocal line is simple: "Sie ist ein Mädchen" ("She is a girl"):

But the orchestra tells us much more. It clothes each note of this phrase in a different and rather outlandish harmony: "boyish hair-do":

mannish jacket:

masculine trousers and shoes:

The "wild tomboy" aspect of Zdenka's nature is also illustrated by an appropriately frisky orchestral passage:

And then the entire passage is repeated to make sure we do not miss any details:

Zdenka's true, feminine essence is characterized by a very different musical equivalent—a much more willowy and timid chromatic passage [13]. But that is not all. Zdenka also happens to be tender, loving, and generous to a fault. She is mortally afraid that Matteo will commit suicide if he is rejected by Arabella. This protective aspect of Zdenka's personality rates still another very special theme [14].

Zdenka writes love letters to Matteo and makes him believe that they come from Arabella. When Matteo comments on Arabella's coldness and indifference when he approaches her, Zdenka tries to attribute it to Arabella's maidenly shyness. "Girls are like that," Zdenka assures Matteo. "A girl wants to give more and more; only she does not want to admit it, and she is dreadfully ashamed of showing it." The instrumental accompaniment to Zdenka's words makes it clear that she is really describing herself, not Arabella. The themes of the girl:

the disguised girl:

the timid girl and the generous girl:

are all combined contrapuntally and present a true-to-life portrait of Zdenka {15}.

If Matteo could understand the language of the Strauss orchestra, he would immediately realize that the "girl" in question is not Arabella, but Zdenka. Alas, Matteo is misled by appearances and words, and does not sense the truth so clearly revealed by the instruments of the orchestra. Zdenka will do anything to prove to Matteo that Arabella loves him. And, as we discover in the last act, she really does *anything* and *everything*. In the introduction to the last act—while the curtain is mercifully closed—we eavesdrop on the passionate love encounter between Zdenka and Matteo. While Matteo believes that the girl he is embracing so ardently in the pitch-black hotel room is Arabella, Strauss combines and recombines the various motives of the real and imagined participants. Such contrapuntal elaborations are among the chief glories of Strauss's operas. But they also have certain less desirable side effects. The polyphonic orchestra tends to engulf the voices and to obscure the enunciation of the words, making it difficult for the singers to project their lines. Strauss was by no means unaware of this problem. For his opera *Intermezzo*, which dealt with an incident from his own life, Strauss wrote the words as well as the music and fashioned the most transparent and subdued orchestration. As he said in the preface to *Intermezzo*, "The devil himself has put orchestral counterpoint into the cradle of German composers in order to curse their operatic life."

Since in the introduction to the last act of *Arabella*, Strauss did not have to worry about words and vocal lines, he could indulge himself in a truly breathless and monumental contrapuntal orgy. He takes two of Zdenka's themes and combines them {16}. Then he takes two of Matteo's themes:

one of Arabella's:

and one of Zdenka's:

and puts all four of them together [17].

The plot presents a very complicated erotic misunderstanding, but eventually everything turns out happily. The trouser-wearing sister who pretended to be a boy proves to be more feminine than the gorgeous goddess who cold-bloodedly played "cat-and-mouse" with her many admirers while awaiting the arrival of her Prince Charming. Near the end of the opera, Arabella sings to Zdenka what is probably the most important sentence of the entire opera: "Zdenkerl, you are the better of us two. You have taught me a good lesson: we should not weigh, bargain, or keep back anything, but keep giving and loving, always" [18].

BORIS GODUNOV

by Modest Moussorgsky

Broadcast February 25, 1978   Cassette illustrations 19–29

Boris Godunov is surely the most Russian of all Russian operas. In its vast panorama of Russian history, Moussorgsky's masterpiece depicts not only the life story of Tsar Boris Godunov but also introduces—as important stage characters—three Russian tsars who succeeded him on the Moscow throne: Boris's son, Feodor, who reigned for a couple of months after his father's death; the pretender Dimitri, who ruled for the next eleven months; and finally Prince Vassili Shuisky, who organized the murders of Feodor and Dimitri and who reigned for the following four years. If this weren't enough, we also hear a great deal about the two tsars who preceded Boris Godunov. For both Ivan the Terrible and his son, the saintly Theodore, are described at great length by the chronicler Pimen and by Boris himself. An opera that concerns itself with *six* Moscow tsars is certainly a unique specimen of *theatrical* history!

Since I was born in Moscow, all this means more to me than to most other people. Furthermore, I have certain personal reasons for keeping a special place in my heart for the opera. To begin with, Tsar Boris and I share the same first name, and this coincidence was a source of great pride to me when I was a little boy. As is true of many of Pushkin's other creations, most educated Russians know his drama *Boris Godunov* more or less by heart. The sentence "Boris, Boris, everything trembles before you" was quoted to me ever so often and always gave me a feeling of special importance. My identification with that other Boris was spoiled to some extent by the undeniable fact that in Pushkin's drama—and in Moussorgsky's opera—Tsar Boris is a murderer who had sent hired assassins to kill the Tsarevich Dimitri, the little boy who was the rightful heir to the throne. It is true that in other respects Boris Godunov is portrayed as a worthy ruler and a kind father, as a man of strength and wisdom. But what good are these fine qualities when a man is a murderer? As I grew older, the question of Tsar Boris's guilt became a less personal matter to me. Even so, I experienced a feeling of definite satisfaction when I learned that authorities on Russian history have lately come to the conclusion that Boris Godunov was innocent and that little Dimitri most likely died as a result of an accident.

Another reason why the opera occupied a place of honor in my childhood was Feodor Chaliapin. The great Russian basso was a friend of the family and a frequent visitor in our home. Not that we children got to see too much of him. Chaliapin had a towering reputation as a storyteller— he was probably the greatest raconteur in all of Russia. The trouble was that most of his stories were not fit for the ears of children. And so, as soon as dinner was over, my brother and I were sent away to our quarters, and all we heard of Chaliapin's stories were the gales of laughter that emanated from the living room.

For a long time, I pestered Father and Mother to take me to see Chaliapin in *Boris Godunov*, and when I was ten years old, my wish was finally granted. It proved, however, a somewhat different experience from what I had anticipated. I had expected that Chaliapin would be on the stage all along, singing away, plotting the murder, getting elected tsar, fighting with the false Dimitri, and, in general, dominating the situation. But that was not the way it turned out.

In the first scene of the Prologue there was the chorus, and then a man came out and sang a solo with a very pretty ending, as I remember it [19]. I was sure it was Chaliapin, but my parents told me, No, that was not Tsar Boris at all, but some nobleman who told the people that Boris was refusing to be crowned tsar. In the second scene there was much ringing of bells and choral singing, and then Chaliapin finally did come out. He looked splendid indeed in all his regalia, but he sang for about two minutes and then left. There was more ringing of bells and singing by the chorus, but Chaliapin never came out again.

After the Prologue there was a long intermission, and then came the first act. A couple of men sang in the first scene, and, after a shorter intermission, still more people sang in the second scene, but there was not a trace of Tsar Boris. There was another long intermission, and then I fell asleep, and I don't think I ever did hear anything that Chaliapin sang that night except the short monologue in the second scene. Of course all this was very long ago. Since then I have heard the opera dozens of times. I heard Chaliapin several times when I was not asleep, and I have heard many outstanding performers of the role, both in Europe and in the United States.

At the Metropolitan alone, the role of Boris has been entrusted in recent years to such superb interpreters as Pinza, Siepi, Rossi-Lemeni, Hines, George London, and Martti Taalvela, each contributing a great vocal gift and fine individual touches of characterization. Whether the artists sang in Russian, Italian, or English, it has always amazed me that they were able to create a complex and dramatically convincing human being in the few scenes in which Tsar Boris appears on stage.

The singer of the title role has surprisingly few opportunities in the opera. Except for the brief monologue in the second scene and the three abrupt sentences he pronounces outside St. Basil's Cathedral, Boris Godunov has only two appearances in the opera—a great sequence in the second act and a shorter episode in the last act, when he dies. But *while* he is on stage, he is the *absolute center* of attention. Not a second is wasted. Every note he sings, every reaction, every movement, every gesture contributes to our understanding of his personality. I can think of no other leading operatic character who tells us so much about himself in such a short span of time.

The essential image that emerges is of a wise and kind ruler who has committed one single misdeed and who is destroyed by his crime, or rather by his own remorse and guilty conscience. Boris Godunov has the most *sincere concern* for the happiness and prosperity of his realm; he is kind to the common people, such as the nurse or the simpleton; he is relentless and imperious with his fawning, deceitful counsellors, such as Prince Shuisky; he is the most affectionate and solicitous of fathers; he is energetic in combating his enemies; he is deeply religious. But all these exemplary traits are nullified by his feelings of unworthiness and guilt.

To illuminate and emphasize each facet of Godunov's complex personality, Moussorgsky has found the most impressive and precise musical means. The themes related to the character of the tsar can be divided into

three main categories, paralleling the three main divisions of Boris Godunov's personality—Boris the ruler, Boris the father, and Boris the sinner.
These themes are so graphic that they are easy to identify, and most of
them recur often enough to impress themselves upon our memory. Certain
musical phrases are always connected with Tsar Boris's deep concern for
the tribulations of his homeland—for the famines, invasions, and epi-
demics that beset Russia during his reign [20]. Others accompany his ad-
monition to his son not to trust false and selfish counsel [21] and his angry
outburst against the two-faced and treacherous Prince Shuisky [22]. Two
basic themes characterize Boris Godunov as a father. One is the tender
phrase that is always associated with his love for his daughter, Xenia [23],
while the other refers to Boris's son, Feodor, and is one of the loveliest in
the opera. It appears in several variations [24]; one of them occurs when
Boris suffers his fatal attack in the last act and calls for his son.

The most telling and effective musical images are reserved for the
portrayal of Boris the sinner, particularly for the central emotion of the
drama—Boris's feelings of guilt and remorse. One phrase that keeps re-
curring in Boris's great monologue of the second act is built on the ascending scale [25]. This music suggests that all of Russia's troubles are sent as
a punishment for Boris's crime. Another important musical passage refers
to Boris's inability to sleep, a poetic concept that Pushkin borrowed from
Shakespeare's Macbeth, who also "murdered sleep" [26].

The phrase dealing with sleeplessness leads directly to the vision of
the blood-spattered, murdered child [27], which is the emotional and
dramatic climax of the score. The musical portrait of the guilty tsar would
be incomplete without quoting Boris's pathetic appeal for forgiveness in
the inspired prayer that precedes his death [28].

At the end of Boris's death scene, we are left with a feeling of deep
compassion for the tortured, repentant spirit of the unhappy tsar of all the
Russias. To end this scene, Moussorgsky has fashioned a uniquely touching postlude. Two melodic lines [29], one descending from the highest
treble, the other moving up from the deepest bass, seem to form a huge
musical curtain that slowly and solemnly closes over the inanimate body
of Tsar Boris.

CARMEN

by Georges Bizet

Broadcast March 10, 1973   Cassette illustrations 30–37

THE ORIGINAL VERSION of *Carmen* differs in many respects from the usual, conventional *Carmen* that Metropolitan Opera audiences have been listening to for the last 89 years, ever since January 1884, when the opera made its debut in this house. The original version was not much of a success when it was first produced at the Opéra Comique in Paris on March 3, 1875. The story of the opera struck most Paris opera-lovers as coarse and in questionable taste. Some people even accused it of being downright vulgar. To the middle-class subscribers of the Opéra Comique, Lillas Pastia's tavern of the second act, where the gypsy girls entertain the local regimental officers, had the odor and appearance of a house of ill repute.

Marie Galli-Marié, who was the first Carmen and who had been personally coached by Bizet, was considered much too brazen in her acting. Her behavior seemed provocative, unattractive, and unfeminine. It so happens that Carmen, as Bizet imagined her, is one of the earliest representatives of what is known nowadays as the "liberated" woman. The fiery Carmencita is an independent, decision-making member of the gang of smugglers. Her life-style is unsentimental and brash. Her love affairs are her own affair—not controlled by any legal or conventional rules. In the year 1875 this was quite unexpected and shocking! The music also seemed bizarre and much too complicated. The reviews were mostly negative and at best lukewarm.

Although seven years had passed since Paris had witnessed the *Tannhäuser* fiasco of 1868, the echo of that scandal was still reverberating loud and clear; and every French composer who attempted to introduce a slightly unconventional musical style was accused of following the German brand of the "music of the future." The management of the Opéra Comique did its best to keep the public interested in the opera. While it is true that *Carmen* was not an immediate hit after its initial performance, the legend that it was a complete flop is not supported by the facts. After the première, on March 3, *Carmen* continued to be given twice and sometimes three times a week; and it achieved the remarkable total of 35 performances during the Opéra Comique's spring season. The opera was taken up again the next fall and was produced about once a week, until its final showing on February 12, 1876. A work that achieves 47 performances in the first year of its existence can hardly be called a total failure.

When *Carmen* was finally dropped from the repertoire of the Opéra Comique, it was mostly because the attendance was falling off and the administration was losing too much money. The finances of the Opéra Comique at that time were in a rather desperate condition. The company was nearing bankruptcy and was bailed out only by the immense success of the seven performances of the Verdi Requiem, gala events that were conducted by the composer. The monetary success of these guest appearances made people quip that "it took a *requiem* to *revive* the Opéra Comique!" Verdi was the hero of the hour, and Bizet was forgotten.

As far as the Paris producers, critics, and audiences were concerned, *Carmen* had been a mistake and a thing of the past. It took more than seven years for the opera to return to the French capital. During this time Carmencita was busy traveling around the world and being received enthusiastically in Austria, England, and Italy, as well as in Russia, Ireland, the United States, Czechoslovakia, Mexico, and South America. The great German philosopher Friedrich Nietzsche heard the opera in Genoa and fell in love with it. In his letters, he wrote of the furor *Carmen* was creating among the Genoese opera-lovers. According to Nietzsche, the introduction to the last act was the favorite number of the Italians [30]. The Genoa audiences listened to these tunes in rapt silence and always forced the conductor to play the introduction twice or even three times in a row.

The world acclaim eventually persuaded the authorities of the Opéra Comique to give Bizet's opera another chance; and in April 1883 *Carmen* returned to the boards of the opera house where it first saw the light of day. To make the locale of the story less objectionable, Lillas Pastia's tavern was transformed into a chic restaurant filled with elegant guests, and the title role was sung not by a husky-voiced hoyden, but by the well-behaved and greatly overweight lyric soprano Adèle Isaac, who was described by an irreverent critic as "the elephant girl with the voice of a nightingale"!

We welcome today's rebirth of *Carmen*, liberated from all the impurities inflicted on it by well-meaning but no longer relevant improvers. The original version was neglected for a long time, and several sections of it were actually lost. The story of its rediscovery is a fascinating combination of detective work and treasure hunt. *Carmen* was originally performed with spoken lines. In 1883, eight years after Bizet's death, a score was published containing additional recitatives and other changes and omissions made for its Vienna production. In this adjusted and emasculated form it was then sung and played all over the globe as "the world's most successful opera." The alterations were made by Bizet's friend the French composer Ernest Guiraud, who is responsible for some significant changes.

In at least two episodes, the sequence of events did not make sense. One occurred near the beginning of the opera, right after the exit of the children's chorus. As the factory bell is ringing, eight or nine young fellows from among the chorus tenors enter the stage. "Now that the bell has rung," they sing, "the charming girls who work in the tobacco factory will soon return from lunch. And when they arrive we will go after them, whispering words of love." This promise, "en vous murmurant des propos d'amour," is elaborated in several graceful vocal phrases [31]. Listening to this music, one cannot doubt that these amorous tenor cavaliers really mean what they say about "murmuring words of love." But when the eagerly awaited factory girls enter the square to sing their own enchanting cigarette chorus, the amorous cavaliers used to stand mute, as if they had lost their voices, and did not utter a single word, loving or otherwise. Well, it just did not seem possible that Bizet had forgotten what his characters had so eloquently promised to do just a few minutes earlier.

Another puzzling episode took place near the end of the third act. When Escamillo arrives at the smugglers' mountain retreat looking for Carmen, he gets into a heated argument with her lover, Don José. Soon the two men pull their knives and get into a fight, during which Escamillo is nearly stabbed to death. Fortunately, Carmen and a few of the gypsy smugglers return just in time to drag the jealous José away from his victim. After thanking Carmen for saving his life, Escamillo addresses José in a most peculiar manner, saying that since they are now even stephen, each of them having won one encounter, he—Escamillo—is willing to fight the third and deciding match any time it would suit Don José's convenience.

The trouble with this elegant and chivalrous statement is that in the preceding action, as it was printed in the score and always shown onstage, there was only one fight, one single encounter, which was won by Don José and lost by Escamillo. It was simply not conceivable that a famous bullfighter, the very embodiment of Spanish pride and honor, would brag of being even stephen with a rival after a single combat, at the end of which his own life was barely saved by the lucky arrival of a girl.

A comparison with the complete libretto of Bizet's original *Carmen* showed that in the original text the cavaliers *did* murmur appropriately amorous words to the cigarette girls; and, at the end of the third act, there were two elaborate fights between José and Escamillo, the first of which was won by Escamillo, so that his offering to fight the deciding match with José made perfectly good sense. The problem was that the music for these two fairly long sections was not included in Bizet's autograph score, which has always been proudly preserved in the library of the Paris Conservatory, although it was perfectly clear from the numbering of the manuscript pages that the music had been there at one time. Somebody— Ernest Guiraud, perhaps, or someone else—mutilated that priceless score by cutting out eight pages containing the cavaliers' music and fourteen pages of the fight sequence. The search for these missing sections was not at first hopeful. Investigators were told that all the original material of *Carmen* had perished in the great fire that destroyed the Opéra Comique building in 1887.

But eventually things changed. The publishing house of Alkor in the German city of Kassel became interested, and its editors hit upon a real treasure trove. In the archives of the Opéra Comique they found all the authentic orchestral and vocal parts of the original version. They had not been destroyed in the fire after all! And so, in 1964, a score was brought out that presented a complete picture of the original version. It is a score that includes the section with the amorous cavaliers, the complete fight scene, and a great number of other passages that are different from the ones we had been hearing. Now that the original *Carmen* is readily available in published form, it is timely to consider its advantages over the more familiar version. We also cannot help wondering why all the changes were made in the first place.

The new section in the first act where the tenor cavaliers make love to the factory workers [32] is a charming piece of music in its own right, but the advantage of restoring it lies in what it does to the entire scene featuring the cigarette girls, the scene which now becomes a much more important and shapely musical entity. First the girls sing by themselves, next the cavaliers murmur their words of love, and finally both groups join in the culminating ensemble section [33]. This completes and rounds out what formerly was a mere fragment, like a tripod with a single leg. The reason why the two legs of the tripod were cut away is easy to guess. The choral sections of *Carmen* are very extensive and even now offer many problems. It is difficult for us to realize how strange and peculiar this music seemed at first to singers who were totally unfamiliar with it. These wonderfully exciting and smooth-sounding ensemble passages that we take completely for granted are actually much trickier than one imagines. The quarrel chorus of the first act, for instance, goes at breakneck speed and calls for the most concentrated attention to rhythmic values [34]. The smugglers' choruses of the third act abound in passages that for a time seemed unnatural and horrendously difficult. One particularly pesky chromatic passage demands very careful treatment of its descending and ascending half-steps [35].

All this was way above the heads of the French and Viennese choristers of a hundred years ago. We know from reports of contemporaries that there was a near rebellion by the ladies of the Opéra Comique chorus, who complained about all the smoking and fighting they were required to do while singing what was in their opinion impossibly difficult music. This was also true of the male choristers. These cavaliers had enough trouble mastering the music with which they made love to Carmen in the first act. By the time they learned to declare their passion for the prima donna, these amorous tenors had no more energy or learning capacity to murmur words of love to mere cigarette girls.

The original fighting sequence between Carmen's two admirers is an even more important restoration. It not only justifies Escamillo's "even stephen" sentence in the finale of the third act but also adds an altogether new and very important dimension to the role of the glamorous bullfighter. In former productions of *Carmen* it always seemed peculiar—to say the least—that a great matador, whose agility in the bull ring was a crucial attribute of his athletic prowess, should be so easily and quickly defeated by a mere soldier. In the restored third-act encounter, Escamillo dominates the situation. He makes fun of José's clumsiness; he even manages to knock José's knife out of his hands. When Escamillo later has José at his mercy, at the end of the first bout of fighting, he lets him go with a most disdainful remark: "My profession is killing bulls, and after all, I'm a very busy man. I can't waste my time with soldiers." José wins the second time not by being a more skillful fighter but because Escamillo's knife accidentally breaks.

I imagine that the fight was shortened to accommodate the Viennese singers, whose well-fed, pot-bellied physiques did not lend themselves to the prolonged athletic exertions of the original fight scene. Cutting out this exciting section is particularly regrettable since it shortens still further one of the most meager of all leading roles in the entire operatic repertoire. It is true that Escamillo gets to sing the "Toreador Song," which is probably the most famous baritone aria in existence. But otherwise, he is allotted remarkably little music. The noted English opera producer Colonel Mapleson tells in his memoirs that when the opera was about to get its first performance in London, the famous baritone Del Puente refused to sing the part of Escamillo, saying that it was beneath his dignity to accept a role more suited to a chorister.

The two sections I have been describing are not the only ones that are new. Far from it! There are many other choral and orchestral passages that are different from those heard in previous years. The back stage choruses of the last act that describe the progress of the bullfight are quite different and much more varied than they used to be. One of these restored passages, fourteen measures of added music, happens to be among my favorites. This section was left out because Carmen's behavior at this point was thought to be too realistic and sort of vulgar. Near the beginning of the second-act duet between Carmen and Don José, the bugles are heard sounding the retreat:

José interrupts Carmen's dance and tells her that he must now return to the barracks for the night. This makes Carmen boiling mad. She accuses Don José of behaving like a little boy who must jump and run every time his military commanders crack the whip. He pleads with her, saying that, although his duty calls him, his heart is breaking; that he loves her more deeply than any woman he has ever known. It is a most touching avowal [36]. As soon as José finishes this tender confession, Carmen—and these are the fourteen new measures—embarks on a cruel and sarcastic parody of José's amorous phrases. She repeats his words and his music, but distorts them so as to make fun of him. The strings in the orchestra illustrate her actions with exaggerated moans and sighs:

which make it clear that she does not for a moment believe in the sincerity of José's feelings [37]. All this gives Carmen a wonderful chance to show the bitchy side of her character. A hundred years ago an opera singer was expected to act like a lady, no matter what role she sang. Thank the Lord those days are gone forever!

DON CARLO

by Giuseppe Verdi

Broadcast March 26, 1983   Cassette illustrations 38–46

NO OPERA OF Verdi's is as complicated as *Don Carlo*, and none has been revised as many times by the composer. Verdi experts distinguish five different versions; the final one appeared in 1876, fully twenty years after the original concept was completed. Verdi was not happy about all this refashioning, which was necessary to satisfy the different requirements of French and Italian operatic traditions. In this respect, Verdi's feelings were very close to those of the author of the original drama, Friedrich Schiller, who complained that it took him four years to complete his play, during which time his attitude toward various events and characters underwent significant changes.

What first attracted Schiller to this theme was the historical fact that King Philip II of Spain married the French princess Elisabeth of Valois, who had earlied been slated to become the wife of Philip's son, Don Carlos. (*Carlos* is the German and French spelling of the hero's name; it is *Carlo* in Italian.) Embroidering on this rather unusual family relationship, Schiller developed it into a drama of triple unhappiness: that of King Philip, who suspects that his wife and his son are having a love affair; the unhappiness of Prince Carlos, who is still in love with the woman who is now his stepmother; and the unhappiness of Philip's wife, who is unjustly accused of infidelity. To add to this triangular conflict, Schiller introduced another amorous intrigue: The beautiful Princess Anna Eboli—a lady-in-waiting to the queen—falls in love with Don Carlos and is rejected by him. When Eboli becomes aware of Carlos's infatuation with the queen, she decides to take vengeance on both the prince and the queen. Schiller referred to this basic concept as *Ein Familiengemälde in einem fürstlichen Hause* ("A picture of family relations in an Imperial household").

To provide relief from these convoluted, romantic events, Schiller added a second theme, dealing with humanitarian, political, and religious matters. To represent these more general ideas and to portray the struggle between the rigid Spanish conservatism of the sixteenth century and the liberal ideas of his own time, he introduced two other characters: the all-powerful Grand Inquisitor, and Rodrigo, Marquis of Posa. Posa—a noble and independent spirit—is most eager to alleviate the unhappy conditions in the Netherlands, which were then under the domination of Spain. Taking advantage of his friendship with Don Carlos—the young people had attended school together—Posa plans to persuade the prince to go to the Netherlands and inaugurate an era of religious tolerance and national independence. Finding the prince totally immersed in his passion for his stepmother, a passion that is not only hopeless but actually very dangerous, Posa looks for help from the queen.

Posa also becomes involved in an unexpectedly close relationship with King Philip and, on top of all this, is forced to try and extricate Carlos from the consequences of his unfortunate encounter with Princess Eboli. Events soon become so fraught with danger for Don Carlos that to save him Posa is forced to sacrifice his own life. To add to all these complications, Verdi's French librettists, Méry and Du Locle, added still another character, one not present in Schiller's drama; they brought to life Emperor Charles V (father of Philip and grandfather of Carlos) and entrusted him with a crucial role in the dénouement of the plot.

Soon after its publication, Schiller's drama became the target of complaints by literary critics, who felt that the actions and motivations of the Marquis of Posa were illogical, inconsistent, and at best difficult to understand. "How could Posa's sudden emergence as the intimate adviser to King Philip be reconciled with his friendship and affection for Carlos, especially since Posa leaves the prince in the dark regarding the events that led to his new position at court?" "What need was there," the critics also asked, "for Posa's self-sacrifice? Couldn't he figure out a less drastic stratagem to protect Carlos from his father's wrath?" To answer these questions, Schiller wrote twelve articles in the form of letters—*Briefe über Don Carlos*—in which he offered a detailed analysis of Posa's character and of the reasons behind his seemingly contradictory behavior.

According to Schiller, Posa's friendship for Carlos is far less important to him than his crusade for political self-determination and for freedom of religious beliefs and practices. Posa is convinced that these libertarian ideals can be realized only through an enlightened monarch, and he hopes that when Carlos succeeds his father on the Spanish throne, he will be the one to accomplish these goals. In the meantime, Carlos's presence in the Netherlands would serve to mitigate the suffering of that unhappy land and lay the foundation for future changes. Posa's affection for Carlos is real, but it is not his dominant emotion. Carlos is rather the means through which Posa's humanitarian and political dreams can be realized.

Certainly, in the opera, at his first meeting with Carlo, Posa makes clear what is foremost in his mind. "O, my beloved prince," he sings, "the hour has struck. The Flemish people are calling you. Help them. Be their savior!" [38]. And while that solemn, marchlike duet theme that is heard so often in the opera, is of course a pledge of friendship [39], it is also a hymn celebrating humanity's craving for freedom. Or, as the original French text put it so eloquently: "Pour l'amour de la liberté!" [40].

Posa hopes that the queen will be able to persuade Carlo to stop lamenting over his lost love and to leave for Flanders. He is able to arrange a private meeting between Carlo and his stepmother, and the queen promises Carlo that she will plead with her husband to let the prince govern Flanders and recommend that he leave for that country the very next day. But Carlo is so overcome with longing for his erstwhile fiancée that this meeting fails to serve the purpose that Posa had planned for it.

The following episode, on the other hand, the scene in which the king inquires why Posa has returned to Spain, produces some totally unexpected results and in fact leads to a startling change in Posa's strategy regarding the fate of the Netherlands. Questioned by the king, Posa describes in most vivid terms the miserable conditions prevailing in the Netherlands, whose inhabitants are crushed by the iron fists of the Spanish soldiers and are relentlessly oppressed by the agents of the Spanish Inquisition. The king points out that his policies have brought peace and calm to Spain and that he expects to achieve the same favorable results in the Netherlands. Philip's praise of his own peaceful government is totally destroyed by Posa's devastating reply that the peace the king is referring to is the "peace of graveyards." Today this is still the ultimate answer to all dictatorships that claim that their policies create peaceful conditions in their realms.

The reaction of the orchestra to the "graveyard" simile is overwhelming: a terrifying groan gradually dying away to a ghostly murmur [41].

The king's silence encourages Posa to pursue his advantage, and he warns the king not to go down in history as a second Nero. Because Philip seems impressed with his eloquent pleading, Posa begins to imagine that the political and humanitarian reforms so dear to his own heart could perhaps be initiated and carried out by Philip. There would be no need to try to straighten out a love-sick young prince, or wait until Carlo inherits his father's throne. Philip's warning that Posa should beware of the Grand Inquisitor is interpreted by the marquis as one more proof that the king's religious ideas are not so very different from his own. No wonder that, by the end of this scene, Posa is filled with exultation. His dream is becoming a reality! The inscrutable heart of the king is opening to new ideas! An unexpected dawn is appearing in heaven [42]!

But Posa's bliss is of short duration. Philip's pitiless denunciation of the Flemish deputies in the second scene of the second act provides ample proof that Posa was deluded, that the king is inalterably committed to the ideals of the Inquisition. Posa is again forced to rely on the help of Philip's son and heir, but events move too fast. Carlo commits two careless and reckless acts. In the first scene of the second act he permits Princess Eboli to guess that he is in love with the queen; and in the next scene, he publicly challenges his father to put the fate of the Netherlands into his hands and actually draws his sword, threatening the king. Later, Carlo's position becomes even more precarious. In the opening scene of the third act, when Posa is summoned into the king's study, he sees not only that the queen has fainted but that her jewel box has been forced open, revealing a medallion with Carlo's portrait. It is obvious that now only the most drastic measures can still save Carlo's life and enable the prince to fulfill his sacred mission in the Netherlands. Posa therefore decides to prove Carlo's innocence by incriminating himself in all the subversive dealings with the Flemish rebels. Posa realizes that by so doing, he is signing his own death sentence, and he most eloquently expresses this heroic decision during this quartet episode. "What will it matter," he sings, "if one Spaniard perishes, as long as his death can ensure the future happiness of his native land!" It is one of the most impressive and beautiful vocal lines of Posa's entire role [43].

According to Schiller's explanation in one of the twelve articles I mentioned earlier, Posa's death is meant to show, in the most emphatic manner, the extent of a man's dedication to his ideals, and to demonstrate that the pursuit of liberty is more important than life itself! Posa's suicide (for that is certainly what it amounts to) is meant to serve as the ultimate medicine to cure the prince of his debilitating amorous preoccupation. And Posa's self-sacrifice *does* produce the desired effect. In the final scene, as Carlo bids farewell to the queen, he promises her that through his actions in the Netherlands he will erect an imperishable monument to his departed friend [44].

In Schiller's drama Posa dies in vain. Carlo does not leave for Flanders. He is caught by his father in the queen's apartments and is sentenced to perish at the hands of the Inquisition. But the French librettists did not like Schiller's ending. There was a general feeling at the Opéra that piling up too many tragic events was to be avoided and that adding Carlos's death to that of Posa would create too much gloom!

In order to make the ending of *Don Carlo* less tragic, the French librettists resuscitated Emperor Charles V. They took advantage of a legend that the old emperor ordered that his memorial services be celebrated while he was still alive and that he himself was present at the funeral service. He supposedly had an effigy of himself buried with all the pomp befitting a Spanish ruler, but he actually remained in the monastery in the guise of an ordinary monk. The rumors about the false funeral and the actual survival of the emperor were well known, particularly in France, where they had been circulated by Spanish exiles.

The operatic version introduces this idea in the second scene of the first act, when the monks chant that the body of the emperor was reduced to dust and ashes [45]. The actual Charles V—in the person of a monk—prays along with the others, imploring God to forgive him [46]. French audiences in 1867 were expected to catch on to this idea immediately. But to remove any doubt or misunderstanding, Carlo is made to recognize the monk's voice as that of his grandfather. Once the identity of the monk is established, he can fulfill the task for which he has been resuscitated. In the final moments of the opera, the voice of the emperor is heard and is recognized by King Philip and the Grand Inquisitor. The gates of the mausoleum swing open and Carlo escapes into the safety of his grandfather's tomb.

The *raison d'être* of this life-saving operation is to show that Posa did not die in vain. Carlo will, perhaps, at some future time, be able to continue the mission his dead friend had entrusted to him. But such speculations are idle. History books tell us that the Netherlands did not achieve independence from Spain for another 80 years. There is, in fact, very little in the opera that is based on solid historical evidence. That does not matter. Tales of amorous involvements between men and women—whether real or romanticized—have always been the stuff on which theatrical shows have concentrated. There are no fewer than six amorous entanglements in *Don Carlo*: the queen's love for her husband and for her former fiancé; King Philip's love for his wife and his love affair with Princess Eboli; Carlo's hopeless passion for his stepmother; and Eboli's unfortunate longing for Carlo. But there is also a seventh passion, a very rare one in life or in opera—a limitless love of freedom: "L'amour exalté, l'amour de la liberté."

EUGENE ONEGIN

by Peter Tchaikovsky

While staying at his country home, Eugene Onegin is introduced to the widow Larina and her two daughters, Olga and Tatiana. Olga is engaged to Onegin's friend Lensky. The romantically inclined Tatiana soon falls in love with the elegant guest and writes Onegin a passionate love letter. A few days later, he meets her in the park and cautions her not to be so careless in expressing her emotions to relative strangers. A month or so later, at the urging of Lensky, Onegin comes to a celebration of Tatiana's name-day at the Larins' home. Here, the sophisticated Onegin becomes annoyed by the gauche behavior of the guests and gets involved in a silly quarrel with his friend. The infuriated Lensky challenges Onegin to a duel. Early the next morning the two men meet by an old mill, and Lensky is killed.

Several years later, after returning from his travels, Onegin attends a ball in St. Petersburg. Here, to his surprise, he meets Tatiana, who in the meantime has married Prince Gremin and has become a leading member of the Russian aristocracy. Falling desperately in love with the woman whom he earlier rejected, Onegin writes Tatiana, begging to see her. Not receiving an answer, he manages to gain access to the palace of the Gremins, confronts Tatiana, and urges her to run away with him. She tells him that even though she still loves him, she will remain faithful to her husband and sends Onegin away forever.

Broadcast March 24, 1979   Cassette illustrations 47–53

EXCERPTS FROM TCHAIKOVSKY'S *Eugene Onegin* were the first opera selections I heard as a child. As far back as I can remember everyone around me knew the music and the words of this opera, could quote from it extensively, and usually did! Tchaikovsky's honeyed melodies had a great deal to do with this, of course, but an even more important reason was Pushkin, Russia's foremost and best-loved poet, and the fact that *Eugene Onegin* was Pushkin's most widely read and best-known poem.

I was about eight years old when, like most other Russian children, I was made to memorize long passages from Pushkin's poem. I still remember much of it. Its satirical social content escaped me completely at that time, of course. I did not realize that in *Eugene Onegin* the poet exposed in merciless detail the emptiness and wastefulness of Russian life among the leisured classes in the reign of Tsar Nicholas I. I was mostly entranced by the romantic love story and by the sadness of it all. Naturally, Tatiana was my favorite—she was so young, so pale, so terribly in love.

How agonizing it must have been for her to write Eugene that passionate love letter. It was so thrillingly unconventional too—weren't men the ones to make avowals and write love letters revealing their eternal devotion? I had heard the music of the letter scene long before I knew the rest of the opera. Given a living room with a piano and an accompanist, every Russian soprano sang it on the slightest provocation. I loved it, particularly the opening phrase portraying Tatiana's feverish yearning [47], then the breathless, interrupted gasps:

building up to an almost intolerable suspense:

and finally the soprano's romantic declaration: "Even though I should perish, I will first yield to that blinding ray of hope and drink the magic poison of desire!" [48].

As a boy, I thought that was tremendously romantic. However, I still remember the shock when for the first time I heard a complete performance of *Eugene Onegin* at the Moscow Opera House. There was the baritone, Eugene, deciding in the last act that he was in love with Tatiana after all, and to my enormous surprise, he sang the music of her letter scene with practically the same words, exclaiming that he was also hoping to drink the "magic poison of desire" [49]. Somehow I could not forgive Tchaikovsky for not composing a different aria for the baritone; this one, I felt, should have been left the sole property of Tatiana!

The next phase of my infatuation with the music of *Eugene Onegin* centered on a very special trick Tchaikovsky has of connecting the individual phrases of his melodies by little ornamental bridges—most appealing, jeweled garlands of musical passages that provide a kind of conversation between the singers and the orchestra. Although Tchaikovsky is willing to entrust these brief interludes to any instrument of the orchestra, he shows a definite preference for the woodwinds, particularly for the clarinet, which flits, every now and then, like an irridescent butterfly from the end of one phrase to the beginning of the next one.

The tenor aria of the second act provides a charming example of this playful technique. The tenor intones the melancholy question: "What will tomorrow hold in store?"

and as soon as he comes to the end of his sentence, a nimble clarinet figure interrupts him, takes the melody away from him, and connects the theme to its next phrase:

The tenor continues with his second sentence:

but the clarinet, which was lying in ambush, waiting for its next opportunity, picks things up immediately:

and brings us to the tenor's third phrase:

Now it's the oboe's turn:

then the flute's and the bassoon's, and we finally are back to the dialogue between the tenor and the clarinet:

Occasionally, this game is played by the orchestra alone, as in the important part of the letter scene when Tatiana is busy penning her letter to Onegin. The oboe carries the opening main part of the melody, but its last two notes are imitated and carried on by the flute, the clarinet, and the French horn [50]. On countless occasions the connecting bridges of the instrumental interludes simply pick up the endings of the vocal melodies and imitate them, as if some instrument of the orchestra is trying to say, "Me too!"

I always find it so touching when, at the end of Tatiana's passionate outburst to her nurse:

the clarinet intones its little complaining echo!

Sometimes we hear a double echo, as in the first scene, when the poet, Lenski, confesses his love for Olga. The tenor phrase ends on four tones, which are echoed twice, first by the flutes and oboes and then by the French horns [51].

Although these echoes are always charming, I much prefer the independent interludes where one never knows just what kind of surprise the connecting passage holds in store, as in the letter scene, where Tatiana's anguished query, "Are you an angel standing by me? Are you a tempter sent to try me?" is answered by the full-bodied phrase of the French horn [52].

It was only many years later, when I had a chance to stage and conduct *Eugene Onegin* in Boston, that I noticed an aspect of its music that had escaped me until then. I had always been impressed with the feeling of unity that this music produced. It all seemed to belong together, as if in some way it had been cut out of the same piece of cloth. Well one day, when working on the score, it suddenly dawned on me that a surprising number of the melodies of the opera did indeed have a common denominator and did belong in a way to the same family. They have a tendency to start with the same three tones, beginning on the third note of the scale and then coming down. It is quite a revelation, when one hears these different tunes, all beginning:

The composer makes no effort to relate such a 3−2−1 tune to any one character in the opera. All of them get their share of the treatment.

The theme associated with the old nurse belongs to this category, even though in its continuation it sounds just like an authentic Russian folk tune:

The hero of the opera, Onegin, can claim quite a collection of melodies, all of which start with the same descending scale pattern. One is his patronizing lecture to Tatiana, in which he so politely explains to her why he can't reciprocate her love:

When he arrives at his duelling appointment, the woodwind melody that accompanies him not only begins with these three notes but also closes with them:

Onegin's entrance to the splendid ballroom in the last act is introduced with still another musical phrase, which, although it seems a little more melancholy, still begins with the same three notes:

When the curtain rises on the second act, the orchestra intones one of the main themes of the opera, which also belongs to this 3−2−1 family. It is, of course, the same theme as in the letter scene, when Tatiana wonders whether Onegin is an "angel standing by her or a tempter sent to try her":

At the end of the next scene, in the tumultuous excitement provoked by the duelling challenge, Tchaikovsky invents still another tune beginning with the same pattern:

So far, we have looked only at the major side of this picture. Quite a few tunes begin with the minor third:

such as Lensky's lament, which I have already mentioned in connection with the clarinet interludes:

In the suspenseful moment just before the two adversaries raise their duelling pistols, there is an interesting variation of this idea. The duel is to begin when one of the seconds claps his hands three times. Each time, the orchestra accompanies the signal with an ominous phrase, which is, of course, our old friend:

One of the most touching moments in the final act—when the weeping Tatiana reads Onegin's love letters—is accompanied by a particularly lovely variation of this musical idea in minor:

It was most important for Tchaikovsky to illustrate musically Tatiana's transformation from the inexperienced and impulsive girl of the first two acts into the cool and self-controlled aristocrat of the last one. And so, to accompany her entrance into the glittering St. Petersburg ballroom, the composer invented a courtly and elegant D-flat major minuet tune:

Notice that this serene musical passage still ends with the 3—2—1 refrain in F minor!

I cannot help wondering why this enchanting work by one of the most popular of all composers has not become an established repertoire favorite in the United States. Besides its delightful music, it offers most grateful opportunities for the singing actors and actresses—stellar roles for the soprano and the baritone, for the tenor and the mezzo-soprano. The only explanation I can think of is that the story of the opera is not only unconventional, but in a way quite frustrating for American audiences, who, unlike the Russians, have not been brought up on it since childhood.

The central character is a woman who falls in love with a man, is rejected by him, and marries another man. She remains loyal to her husband, even though she still loves the first man, who now belatedly discovers that he is in love with her, after all. This plot, while unusual, is not by itself untheatrical. Operatic literature has quite an assortment of wives who love other men. As a rule, it ends tragically, with the woman's death, as with Isolde or Mélisande; sometimes the husband kills the unfaithful wife's lover, as in Puccini's *Il Tabarro*; sometimes the husband kills both his wife and her lover, as in *Pagliacci*. Faithful wives who remain faithful, even though they love other men, are extremely scarce in opera, but Tatiana is not the only one. Another wife who chooses to fight her guilty love is Amelia in Verdi's *Ballo in Maschera* (The Masked Ball). Observe, however, the difference in dramatic treatment: In *The Masked Ball*, Renato, the husband, discovers his wife's infatuation and refuses to believe in her innocence. At first he wants to kill her, but then decides to kill the man who alienated his wife's affections. This is the sort of thing that we have come to expect in stories dealing with conflicts of amorous passion. But, in

Eugene Onegin, the husband remains blissfully unaware of his wife's emotional dilemma. Prince Gremin is definitely the least formidable of operatic husbands. He appears in only one scene, in the last act, and sings a lovely aria, telling his rival how much he is in love with his own wife; and that is the first and the last we see of him. On the surface, the plot gives the impression of following the lines of the well-known love triangle, but it is completely lacking in fireworks and bloodshed.

In the final scene Tatiana tells Eugene that she indeed was in love with him, that she still loves him, but that she has chosen to remain faithful to her husband. They even sing a kind of love duet, reflecting that happiness was once "so near and so possible" [53]. In spite of Eugene's passionate pleading, Tatiana leaves the scene, and the final curtain falls after a single sentence, culminating again in a 3−2−1 minor cadence wherein the spurned admirer laments his former blindness. This inconclusive ending leaves us wondering. Will Onegin keep on courting Tatiana and try to win her? Will he eventually marry another girl? Or will he remain a bachelor to the end of his days, lamenting his lack of sense when he rejected the girl who threw herself at his feet?

Tchaikovsky, by the way, was quite aware that this ending was, dramatically speaking, dangerous, and he quite seriously considered having Tatiana leave her husband and run away with Onegin. He could not, however, bring himself to change the character of Pushkin's heroine and incur the anger of thousands of readers who loved Tatiana just as the poet portrayed her. And herein, perhaps, lies the secret of popularity of all operatic works: We have learned to know, to pity, and to love the Carmens and Aïdas, the Rodolfos and Alfredos, the Isoldes and Leonoras. Let us hope that Tchaikovsky can bring Tatiana and Onegin and Lensky and Olga closer to our hearts!

FALSTAFF

by Giuseppe Verdi

Broadcast April 1, 1972   Cassette illustrations 54–66

V ERDI's FALSTAFF is enormously admired by most conductors, stage directors, musicologists, composers, and instrumentalists; but in spite of all this admiration, this work is performed far less often than the same composer's *Otello*, *Don Carlo*, *Un Ballo in Maschera*, or *La Forza del Destino*; not to mention such perennial Verdi favorites as *Aïda*, *Traviata*, *Rigoletto*, or *Trovatore*. And so it is rather intriguing to search out the cause of this strange discrepancy between high regard in high places and a rather low number of productions and performances. One reason for this, I believe, is that *Falstaff* is primarily an ensemble piece, and the individual singer has less than the usual chance to display the splendor of his or her voice and the extent of its vocal range.

Of course, this is not quite true of the male contingent. Certainly the fat knight, Jack Falstaff, who is the hero of the drama, has his full share of effective vocal solos, for example, his great monologue in the opening scene dealing with Honor, which is borrowed from Shakespeare's *King Henry the Fourth*. In the second scene of the second act, he has another outstanding solo bit: a very short but delightful arietta in which the monstrously fat fellow tries to impress Alice Ford with the fact that at one time, when he was a young lad and "When he was page to the Duke of Norfolk":

Quan-d'e-ro pag - gio del Du-ca di Nor-folk

"He was so graceful, elegant, and nimble that he could have squeezed himself into a thimble":

Che sa-rei guiz-za - to at-tra-ver-so un a - nel - lo.

Falstaff sings still another big aria at the very beginning of the third act, the aria which ends with the famous eulogy to good wine and its beneficial effects on the human psyche.

The leading tenor, Fenton, also has a lovely solo at the beginning of the final scene. And certainly, the other leading man, Alice Ford's jealous husband, has no reason to complain, since he has what is undoubtedly the prize solo piece of the opera. His aria in the first scene of the second act is known by its opening words: "E sogno o realtà?" ("Is it a dream or reality?") Among its many other virtues is its wonderful climax, in which Ford sings the praises of jealousy: "Laudata sempre sia nel fondo del mio cor la gelosia!" ("From the bottom of my heart, God be praised for my jealousy!") [54].

But, on the other hand, Verdi has treated the four leading ladies of the opera very unkindly. All of them are required to sing a great deal of most exacting music, but hardly anything suitable for purely vocal display. What is particularly surprising is that the composer has given neither the leading soprano, Alice Ford, nor the leading contralto, Dame Quickly, a single aria—*not one* extended section of music that can be extracted from the role and sung as a separate concert or display piece! Of the four female roles—and Lord knows all four require artists of the highest vocal, musical, and histrionic gifts—only Nanetta has anything that can be described as a regular recitative and aria: "Sul fil d'un soffio etesio," and even she has to wait until the final scene of the opera to sing it [55].

Most opera lovers are familiar with the opening lines and tunes of dozens of Italian soprano arias, but I wonder how many know either the opening words or the tune of Nanetta's song. This is not a matter of indifference, for arias sung by leading sopranos and contraltos have an important bearing on the popularity of an opera. One only has to consider the enormous appeal of such Verdi arias as Gilda's "Caro nome," Azucena's "Stride la vampa," Aïda's "Ritorna vincitor," Leonora's "Pace, pace," or Desdemona's "Willow song" and "Ave Maria" to realize how much these excerpts contribute to the fame of the operas in which they occur. Audiences are not the only ones whom the composers of operas have to please. There are also the prima donnas themselves, who like to have arias that exhibit their vocal gifts. And leading-lady vocalists have been known to be quite vocal about their vocal desires. We know that Bizet had to write several versions of the Habanera before Galli-Marié, the first Carmen, was satisfied with it. Nor did Puccini get away with the notion that the dramatic continuity of *Tosca* did not have a logical and appropriate place for a soprano aria. "Vissi d'arte" had to be added to the score at the last moment—much to the composer's chagrin—or else the beautiful Miss Darclée, the first Floria Tosca, would have been "much too unhappy" to do a good job in the first performance.

But while all this is true enough in general terms, it does not apply in the case of *Falstaff*. Verdi was 76 years old when he started writing this opera, and at this point in his life and fame, he did not have to please either audiences or prima donnas. *Falstaff* was written to please only Verdi himself, and as far as he was concerned, it was only Papa Shakespeare, as Verdi called him, who had to be considered and paid attention to. From Shakespeare's point of view, the gist of the drama consists of one grand contest between the enormously fat and equally conceited knight and the ensemble of citizens of Windsor, who are led by the two merry wives, Mistress Ford and Mistress Page.

It is true that redesigning Shakespeare's *Merry Wives of Windsor* to fit the format of an Italian opera was by no means an easy task. But, fortunately, Verdi was helped by a most skillful and dedicated collaborator, by far the most brilliant of all Italian librettists, Arrigo Boïto. Even though Boïto found it desirable to include a few passages from Shakespeare's *King Henry the Fourth*, he still succeeded in compressing the five acts and twenty-two scenes of the *Merry Wives* into an opera having only three acts and six scenes. Furthermore, he managed to reduce Shakespeare's sixteen male characters to a mere seven: three tenors and four basses and baritones.

This called for rather drastic surgery. In the process Boïto had to amputate Meg's sensible and trusting husband, Mr. Page, and give Shakespeare's "sweet Anne Page" a new set of parents, making her the Fords' daughter, Nanetta. Nanetta also lost one of her silly suitors, leaving her only the ridiculous Dr. Cajus to contend with. Even Falstaff lost one of his swashbuckling sharpsters and was left only Bardolf and Pistol. Shakespeare's three punishments of Falstaff were reduced to two, and, in the process, we lost the rollicking scene in which Falstaff receives a nasty trouncing while he masquerades as Mother Pratt, the fat woman of Brentford. But all the basic groupings remain intact. In the second scene of the first act there are still four women plotting against Falstaff while five men discuss Falstaff's intention to seduce Alice Ford. There are still the two hilarious invitation scenes in which Dame Quickly flatters Falstaff into believing that Alice Ford would be most anxious to be seduced by him; and the love intrigue between Nanetta and Fenton is the same as in Shakespeare.

Happily, Boïto has retained what is certainly one of the most amusing situations in the entire theatrical repertoire, the first scene of the second act, in which a jealous husband argues most eloquently to achieve the seduction of his own wife and then realizes to his horror that he can now look forward to his own imminent cuckolding and behorning of his own forehead. In this scene between Falstaff and Ford, masquerading under the name of Fontana, we can observe Verdi's special technique of ensemble work—the sharing and dividing of vocal lines. Even the most personal melodic phrases, which in earlier Verdi operas would have been automatically composed as solo utterances, are shared among several singers. Thus when Ford-Fontana tells Falstaff how he serenaded Mistress Ford, his madrigal tune is constantly interrupted and carried on by Falstaff [56].

The other musical technique employed so masterfully in this opera is the *big ensemble*, in which many participants sing simultaneously, and yet each character sings special characteristic vocal lines. This type of vocal ensemble has always been a Verdi specialty. We know it well from such famous examples as the Quartet from *Rigoletto*, where all four characters sing of love in their own special way: the Duke makes passionate love to Maddalena; Maddalena flirts and giggles, responding to the Duke; Gilda sobs brokenheartedly at seeing the Duke being unfaithful to her; and Rigoletto's lines express a father's love for his suffering daughter. After being presented separately, these vocal lines are then sung simultaneously.

In *Falstaff*, Verdi has gone a step further. The characters not only sing individual lines that are in keeping with their personalities but also congregate in groups that themselves are handled as musical entities. In the second scene of the first act, there is a remarkable example of this group ensemble technique. The four women start the scene by sharing and dividing individual lines [57]. Next, they join as a unit in a group song, singing in triplets, three notes to a beat [58]. Then the five men, after conversing individually, join together, singing four notes to a beat [59]. Near the end of the scene, these two groups—the tripletting women and the quadrupling men—are made to sing at the same time. The tenor, Fenton, is then separated from the rest of the men and given a lovely melody consisting of long notes [60]. To crown this wonderful scene, the gossiping women, the chattering men, and Fenton, all singing together, create the most exquisite ensemble.

An even more extraordinary combination of alternating and simultaneous ensembles occurs in the second scene of the second act, where the plot provides four different groupings. The two young lovers, Nanetta and Fenton, who take refuge behind the screen form one group. Nanetta's father, Ford, who is convinced that the amorous couple hiding behind the screen consists of his wife and Falstaff, urges his supporters to surround the screen so as to prevent the escape of the guilty wife and her lover. This collection of angry men, consisting of Ford, Dr. Cajus, Bardolf, Pistol, and various neighbors, constitutes the second group.

On the opposite side of the stage is the laundry basket, in which Falstaff is hiding from the jealous husband. Dame Quickly and Meg Page, who are busy piling dirty linen on Falstaff, make up the third grouping of the ensemble; while Falstaff, who is afraid of choking to death under the dirty clothes, contributes the fourth and last element of the musical construction. The real lovers, Nanetta and Fenton, sing a sustained melody:

the women contribute triplets:

the men give out with the more excited quadruple rhythm:

and finally Falstaff interjects his occasional moaning complaints: "I'm stifling, I'm choking." The total effect is a multifaceted, harmonious, and most ingenious musical piece {61}.

This new approach to ensemble writing enabled Verdi to create a very personal type of continuous drama permeated with music. Of course, speaking of music dramas always makes one think of Richard Wagner, but there is a profound difference between Verdi's and Wagner's treatment of dramatic verities in opera. In Verdi's *Falstaff*, in spite of all the instrumental subtleties, the emphasis is still very much on the stage and the singers. By the end of his career, Verdi was looking for uninterrupted theater, in which the singing actors would collaborate with, and be inspired by, each other, rather than showing off their individual gifts. Even when Verdi gives a singer an exciting aria, he does not permit it to become a show stopper, and he carefully plans to break down the applause or even prevent it from arising. Not only is there no full stop in the orchestral continuity, but at the end of an aria, Verdi immediately brings on new characters. By introducing new situations, he prevents the drama from coming to a halt or from staggering along in spurts and starts. In the first scene of the second act, for instance, at the end of Ford's great monologue praising jealousy, there is a very quick transition to the return of Falstaff. The dramatic and musical situation is so amusing that even the most enthusiastic standee has to refrain from applauding in order to watch and listen to the new development {62}. Similarly, Fenton's aria in the last scene of the opera does not come to a vocal climax, but dissolves into a duet with Nanetta. The two of them unite their voices in a lovely passage that has already been heard twice in the second scene of the first act {63}.

Another reason why *Falstaff* is so beloved by composers and conductors is that in this work, more than in any preceding one, Verdi delights in unusual musical effects. He displays a marvelous inventiveness in the use of harmonic changes and progressions. I would like to illustrate this with two examples of which I happen to be particularly fond. One occurs in the final scene of the opera, when Falstaff arrives at midnight in Windsor Park for his rendezvous with Mistress Ford. When the church bell offstage strikes twelve times to indicate the midnight hour, each stroke of the chime, which is tuned to F natural, is harmonized in a different manner. Starting with a simple F major chord, we get twelve separate harmonizations, all based on the same note. The progression ends back in F major when Falstaff finally confirms, after counting each ring, that midnight has arrived {64}.

The other example of a most unusual sequence of chords occurs at the end of Falstaff's third-act aria, when he describes the thrilling effects of good wine. After the wine passes the lips, says Falstaff, it begins to vibrate. First it warms the cockles of the heart, and then, little by little, the throbbing spreads out far and wide until the whole world ends up pulsating. This idea of a gradually spreading vibration is illustrated in the orchestra by a trill that begins on E natural played by a single flute. It is then taken up by all the other instruments, traveling through a succession of many unrelated keys—A major, F major, A-flat major, F minor, E-flat major, and others—until the entire orchestra, including all the strings, woodwinds, and brasses, vibrates and trills in the key of E major {65}.

But of course the most surprising and delightful invention in *Falstaff* is its final Fugue, in which all the characters in turn present the moral of the play: "Tutto nel mondo e burla. L'uom e nato burlone, burlone, burlone!" ("Everything in the world is a joke. Man was created to laugh and to be laughed at!") [66]. Blessed are those who laugh. Equally blessed are those who are laughed at. But most blessed of all are those who, like Falstaff, can laugh at themselves!

THE FLYING DUTCHMAN

by Richard Wagner

Broadcast January 27, 1968   No cassette illustrations

T HE LAST ACT OF *The Flying Dutchman* opens with an extended and very lively choral scene consisting of three separate episodes: first the singing and dancing of the recently arrived Norwegian sailors, next their conversation with a large group of local girls, and finally—after the girls leave— an interplay between the Norwegians and the ghostly crew of the Dutchman's ship. Besides being a superb example of Wagner's skill in constructing complicated choral ensembles, this scene reveals the full scope of his talents as a practical stage director and producer. His operatic versatility is truly impressive. Not content with being the librettist and the composer, Wagner also gives explicit directions regarding the scenic arrangements as well as the lighting and technical effects.

> It is a clear, bright night, and on the rocky shore the two ships [Daland's and the Dutchman's] are moored fairly close to each other. The Norwegian ship is gaily illuminated. Its sailors are on deck, and there is much jubilation and merrymaking. The appearance of the Dutch ship presents a weird contrast. It is enveloped in unnatural gloom and deathly silence. Later in the act, when the Dutch sailors are heard singing from the bowels of their ship, dark-blue flames begin to glow on the deck; a dreadful gale blows and howls through its naked rigging, and the vessel itself is tossed up and down by the waves. All this, however, happens only in the immediate vicinity of the Dutchman's ship. Otherwise, the sea and the air remain completely calm.

Besides being picturesque, all these details in Wagner's own stage directions intensify one of the central ideas of the drama, namely, the musical and visual contrast between the robust naturalness of the Norwegians and the supernatural ghostliness of everything related to the person and the ship of the Dutchman. In the first two acts this idea is carried mainly by the Dutchman himself and by such spooky scenic effects as the completely silent, phantomlike sailing and docking of the Dutchman's ship. In the third act, this eerie confrontation is developed on a much larger scale.

The scene begins with a brisk and boisterous C-major chorus by the Norwegians:

Not content with singing, the sailors soon break into a dance, and here Wagner finds it useful to put on still another hat, that of the choreographer. He directs the dancing sailors to indicate the downbeat of each measure with a heavy stomping of their feet.

At this point the girls of the town appear carrying food and drink. Seeing the sailors cavorting, the girls cannot refrain from dropping a few slightly sarcastic remarks: "Just look there, how they jump and prance. They don't need us to make them dance!" The sailors stop their twirling and stomping and ask the girls where they are going with all those refreshments. "We must show some hospitality to the strangers, your neighbors there!" say the girls, but when they approach the other ship, they are surprised that there are no signs of life. The ship appears to be deserted. "Hey, sailors" the girls shout, "attention please, give us some lights. It's dark out here!" The Norwegian sailors find this new development quite amusing: "Ha, ha, ha!" they say, "don't wake them up! They're fast asleep." The girls do not pay any attention to the Norwegians' teasing and keep on calling to the Dutchman's crew: "Hey, sailors, hey! Answer us, please!"

The stage direction in the score at this point says *Grosse Stille* ("long and complete silence")! But that is Wagner the librettist speaking. Wag-

ner the musician wants to represent this brooding silence by a more posi-
tive means than an absence of sound. And so he creates a sort of echo, but
not a natural resounding of the healthy and vigorous C-major call of the
girls. And so amidst this "grosse Stille"—the great silence that follows
the clanging fortissimo C major of the full orchestra and the young voices:

we hear a muffled, sepulchral C-sharp minor triad played *pianissimo* by two
French horns and a bassoon:

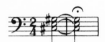

Even to our modern ears, jaded by twentieth-century refinements in ca-
cophonous dissonances, this succession of keys sends a shiver down our
spinal cords. What follows next is really quite witty, and it is a shame that
words sung by choral groups are so difficult to distinguish, no matter how
clearly they are enunciated. Seeing the girls standing there with all that
food in their hands, the Norwegian sailors decide to tease them a bit
more. "Watch out," they say, "they are not sleeping; they are dead." The
girls ignore their countrymen and continue to try to rouse the strangers:
"Hey, sailors, get up! Don't be lazy. It's time to be merry, it's time to be
gay!" The Norwegian sailors interrupt them again, with "Watch out, it is
a dragon's lair. The dragons hide their treasure there!" Isn't it amazing
that the first mention of the dragon who hides in his lair, guarding his
treasure—the dragon who makes his full-dress appearance many years
later as Fafner in the third drama of the Nibelung cycle—is made by Norwegian sailors in a libretto written by Richard Wagner when he was 27
years old?

The girls make two more attempts to rouse the Dutch sailors, but
after the ghostly echo answers them for the third time, they become dis-
couraged and even a bit scared: "No answer? Well, it seems they're dead!"
Their friends on the Norwegian ship now decide to try a new tack: "Of the
Flying Dutchman you've heard the tales. You heard of his ship with the
blood-red sails." The girls object to this, saying: "You must be quiet, you

must be still. Of the dead and of ghosts you must speak no ill!" And here Wagner decides to use a detail imagined by the German poet and writer Heinrich Heine, whose description of the Dutchman legend provided the basis for Wagner's opera. The description is found in Heine's story "The Memoirs of Herr von Schnabelewopski":

> When the Dutchman's ship meets another ship, some of the unearthly sailors come in a rowboat and beg the others to take a packet of letters home for them. These letters are always addressed to people whom no one knows, and who have long been dead, so that some late descendant gets a letter addressed to a far-away great-great-grandmother, who has slept for centuries in her grave.

Using this idea of Heine's, Wagner makes the Norwegians address the Dutchman's crew with the words: "Have you written some love letters while you were afloat? For our grandmothers or great aunts a greeting or a note?" To which the girls reply: "Their girlfriends can't read; their eyes are closed. Within their graves they found repose." Finally, seeing that the crew of the strangers' ship cannot be roused, the girls give all their refreshments to their countrymen on the friendly ship and leave, promising to return later to dance with the sailors. The Norwegians, delighted with all the food and drink they have unexpectedly inherited from their neighbors, become ever noisier and rowdier. They challenge the strangers to join in their singing: "Come out, good friends, and have no fear. The girls are gone; the coast is clear!" At last they forget all about their neighbors and return to their first C major ditty. They do not notice that the sea around the Dutchman's ship is beginning to boil and its masts are shaking in the wind.

The commotion around the Dutchman's ship and in the orchestra gradually grows in intensity. Just as the Norwegians are preparing to resume their twirling and stomping, they become aware of the frightening events on the other side of the shore. The music shifts from the friendly key of C major to B minor, the classical key of death. Now the song of the phantom sailors emerges full-blown from the hull of the Dutchman's ship:

Here again Wagner shows his flair for technical details by indicating

that the voices of these invisible singers should be amplified by special
funnel-shaped megaphones. The song that is thus amplified tells the story
of the Dutchman's cursed destiny: "Now that seven years have past, go
ashore, oh, captain brave; go and find a bride at last, true and faithful to
the grave!" Hearing this, the Norwegians are struck with terror, but decide to keep up their courage by repeating their own song. This provides
the motivation for the final and most elaborate section of this choral scene.
Wagner shows his great musical skill by presenting the music of both the
Dutch and the Norwegian sailors at one and the same time. Eventually
the horrified Norwegians leave the deck of their ship, making the sign of
the cross. This provokes a burst of satanic laughter from the ship on the
other side of the bay. There is a *fortissimo* crash in the orchestra, and suddenly the sea and air become calm again and the former silence and gloom
settle on the Dutchman's ship. The transition to the next scene is provided
by the final appearance of the unearthly echo:

This short analysis demonstrates the great importance Wagner attached to every detail of his choral scenes. He was, of course, even more
concerned with the behavior of his leading characters and with their abil-
ity to act out and do justice to the main ideas of his music dramas. Being a
man of great practical experience, Wagner was keenly aware that the run-
of-the-mill opera singers of his time had neither the training nor the desire to bring out in full the dramatic values that were so all-important to
him. As long as he could personally supervise the production of his works,
Wagner felt reasonably certain that he could teach, cajole, or force the
singers to do justice to his ideas. Unfortunately, he had equally excellent
reasons to believe that with other producers, the results could turn out to
be disastrous. When Wagner had to leave Germany after the revolutionary
disturbances of 1848, his concern for the fate of his operas became particularly acute. Unable to be present at the rehearsals of *The Flying Dutchman*,
he did the next best thing. He published elaborate instructions to acquaint singers and directors with his precise wishes regarding the execution of this work. Like every good director, Wagner was particularly concerned with the behavior of his principal singers at times when they were
not singing. He wanted to be sure that their movements would be prop-

erly coordinated with the music of the orchestra. When a musical passage was meant to illustrate the movements of a certain character, Wagner wanted the singer playing the role to realize its significance and act with great precision. In his pamphlet "Remarks on the Execution of *The Flying Dutchman*," Wagner took great pains to explain just how he wanted them to move, and how much importance he attached to their acting. Here, for instance, is his description of the first appearance of the leading baritone:

> During the deep trumpet notes at the very end of the introductory scene, the Dutchman comes ashore along a plank lowered by one of the crew. His rolling gate, typical of a sailor when he first steps on dry land after a long voyage, is accompanied by a wavelike figure in the cellos and the violas. With the first quarter note of the third measure, he takes his second step, always with folded arms and eyes fixed in the distance. . . . With the repetition of the words "dies der Verdamnis Schreckgebot," the Dutchman drops his head and shoulders and remains in this position through the first four measures of the postlude; with the tremolo of the violins he lifts his face; with the muffled kettledrum roll he begins to shudder—his downturned fists are clenched convulsively, his lips begin to move, and, at last, with eyes fixed heavenward, he starts to sing.

In describing the exit of Senta's father, in the middle of the second act, Wagner again goes into great detail:

> The entire postlude of Daland's aria must be acted out with great precision. Daland turns to leave without further ado, but then he stops and turns around, so that at the next statement of his theme and during the following seven measures, he can—half-pleased and half-expectant—watch, now the Dutchman, now his daughter. With the next two measures for the double basses, he goes to the door and opens it, shaking his head. But with the resumption of his theme in the horns and the bassoon, he thrusts his head in once more, withdraws it vexedly, and with the F-sharp major chord, disappears for good. The Dutchman and Senta remain alone and stand motionless in contemplation of each other.

Wagner's observations on the general character of the different roles in *The Flying Dutchman* are equally fascinating, and the intensity of his feelings is often reflected in the almost frantic tone of his remarks:

> I beseech the exponent of the role of Daland not to drag this role into regions of low comedy. Daland is a rough and ready sailor who, in his pursuit

of commercial gain, scoffs at storms and dangers. When Daland practically sells his daughter to a rich man, he sees nothing reprehensible or disgraceful in that. He thinks and deals like a hundred thousand others, without the least suspicion that he is doing anything improper.

Of the role of Eric, Wagner writes:

Under no circumstances may Eric be played as a sentimental whiner: on the contrary, Eric is stormy and impulsive and—like every man who lives alone, particularly in northern countries—he is something of an introvert.

The correct interpretation of Eric's last-act aria was a matter of great concern for Wagner:

A tenor who sings the third-act cavatina in a sugary manner would do me a sorry service indeed! This piece must breathe distress and heartache. Anything that might lead to a false conception—such as the high B flat in the middle of the cavatina or the cadenza at the end of it—should, I *implore*, be altered or omitted!

How extraordinary for a composer to suggest that some of his music should, if necessary, be altered or omitted! It is quite obvious from these remarks that, for Wagner, fundamental dramatic character was infinitely more important than any outward musical trappings.

LA FORZA DEL DESTINO

by Giuseppe Verdi

Broadcast February 12, 1972   Cassette illustrations 67–84

T HE CHARACTER OF musical keys is a subject that is quite intriguing in its own right. It has a special fascination for opera lovers, for the theatrical resources of music seem to provide composers with a colorful technique for establishing the mood of a scene and for elaborating the psychological details of the plot.

Let us first see what is really involved here, just in terms of numbers. There are seven keys with sharps, seven with flats, and one without either sharps or flats. Each of these fifteen key *signatures*, as they are called, can designate either a major or a minor mode. So, all in all, there are thirty different keys. Since a composer has a choice of fifteen major and fifteen minor keys, the question is: do all these keys have *different* musical characters?

In the seventeenth and eighteenth centuries musicians developed a very definite attitude toward the meaning of music, an attitude that found its expression in the so-called *Affektenlehre*, a German term that can be roughly translated as "the doctrine of emotions." According to this theory, music expresses definite moods and feelings, depending on whether it is fast or slow, loud or soft, smooth or accented. Also according to this theory, each major and each minor key has a fairly definite function. Some keys are supposedly suitable for tender emotions, some for happiness and exuberance, and others for melancholy feelings or tragedy.

Many of these ideas were abandoned fairly soon, but some have kept their validity, particularly in the more romantic styles of the nineteenth century. For instance, fast, loud, accented music is energetic and exciting. Slow, smooth music is calmer, more sustained, and more lyrical. Major keys are generally gayer and minor keys more melancholy. This permits four basic combinations: a rapid tempo in a major key suggests an energetic and gay mood; fast music in a minor key is likely to be turbulent and unhappy; slow pieces in major keys are usually calm and confident; and sustained, slow music in a minor key is more dejected and melancholy.

Let us apply these very general characteristics to the music of *La Forza del Destino*. First, energetic and gay. Well, there isn't much gaiety, of course, but there is some! In the second act the Italian and Spanish soldiers, who have just won a battle with the Germans, are feeling very pleased with themselves, and along with their camp followers they sing a chorus in praise of the invigorating joys of military life [67]. It is a good example of fast, accented, and loud music in a major key and there is no doubt that it *is* gay and energetic! Examples of rapid tempo in a minor key, of excited and unhappy music, are plentiful in this opera. One of the most turbulent themes, one that occurs over and over, symbolizes the destiny that so relentlessly pursues the heroine [68]. Perhaps to show that Leonora and Alvaro can never escape from the malevolent power of their predestined fate, Verdi presents this theme in many keys; A, E, C sharp, and B flat, but, of course, always in the minor mode. A foreboding, tragic theme of this kind would almost be unimaginable in a major key [69].

A slow tempo coupled with a major key associates itself quite naturally with religious feelings, and there are several such slow devotional pieces in *Forza*. The prayer at the end of the first act, "La vergine degli angeli" ("Our Lady of Angelic Hosts"), is a perfect example of an Adagio in a major key [70]. *Forza* is so richly provided with tragic events that it is difficult to know which slow piece in a minor key is the best example of a melancholy mood. The famous duet between Don Carlo and the wounded Alvaro will serve our purpose as well as any other excerpt. It occurs in the second act and is known by Alvaro's opening lines: "Solenne in quest'ora"—"In this solemn hour I beg you to promise you'll grant me a favor" [71]. It sounds almost like a funeral march.

There are, of course, many exceptions to these general observations. One finds some quite gay pieces in minor keys, especially in a fast tempo, and tragic situations have occasionally been presented in a slow tempo in a major key. In general, however, these characteristic combinations of fast and slow, coupled with major and minor, have been treated fairly consistently by most composers who wrote in the traditional system of tonalities.

Before we continue, I would like to clear up a small side issue which tends to complicate this problem. Certain sections of Italian operas—particularly important arias—are not always performed in the keys in which they were written. When a change is made (the technical name for it is *transposition*), it is usually made to a key a half or a whole tone lower. This transposing is done to accommodate a singer who feels more comfortable in the lower key. Alternative keys for arias are quite often printed in the orchestral parts.

A singer who feels indisposed or is perhaps afraid that he will crack on a high note, may ask the conductor—before the performance begins, or even in the intermission before the coming act—to transpose his aria. When the time comes, the conductor points his finger downward; the orchestra players know what that means and will play the lower version printed in their parts. Occasionally the composer himself will miscalculate and set an aria in a key that all singers of this role find uncomfortable or even unsingable. The most famous example is Don Basilio's "La Calunnia" ("Slander Song"), in Rossini's *The Barber of Seville*. Rossini wrote the aria in D major [72], but no bass in the world can, or wants to, sing it in this key. It is always sung a whole tone lower, in C major [73].

A somewhat similar situation exists in *Forza*. Verdi originally wrote Don Carlo's great aria "Urna fatale del mio destino" ("O fatal secret ruling my destiny") in F major, and that is how it was printed in the first edition of the score. When his leading baritone complained that it was uncomfortably high for him, Verdi transposed the second half of the aria down a half tone, to E major [74]. Eventually, to accommodate other baritones, Verdi gave his permission to transpose the first half of the aria as well. This not only pleases the baritones, but also affects the entire musical image of the role of Don Carlo in relation to the other characters in the drama. I will discuss this aspect of this transposition a little later.

To return to our basic problem, we find that many composers have shown strong predilections for certain keys when dealing with specific moods or dramatic situations. Mozart, for instance, was very fond of connecting an Andante in A major with the idea of young people in love or of innocent girls in danger of being seduced. The most famous example of an Andante seduction in A major occurs in *Don Giovanni*, when the Don almost succeeds in seducing Zerlina in the duet "La ci darem la mano" [75]. Another is in the aria "Crudel! Perché finora," from *The Marriage of Figaro*, which begins in A minor, then changes to A major, as Count Almaviva thinks that he has persuaded Susanna to submit to his extramarital desires [76]. But this is just the beginning! There are beautiful Andante love duets in Mozart's *Idomeneo* and in his *La Clemenza di Tito*. In *Così fan Tutte* there are no fewer than three such A-major Andantes dealing with the subject of young love, one of which is the delicious "Un aura amorosa" [77], in which Ferrando expatiates on his love for Dorabella.

What about other composers you will ask? Do they also think of A major in such Mozartian terms? A surprising number of them do. We find comparable A-major moods in the operas of Rossini, Beethoven, and Weber, as well as in Strauss's *Der Rosenkavalier*. Puccini has several love scenes that feature such A-major moods. There is the ever-popular ending of the first act of *La Bohème* [78], and several A majors in the most elaborate of all Puccini's love scenes, the one between Cio-Cio-San and Lieutenant Pinkerton in *Madama Butterfly* [79].

This particular mood has been charmingly described by still another musician, surprisingly, by the Russian composer Rimsky-Korsakov. I say "surprisingly" because from a Russian we normally would expect comments on more somber and tragic keys than A major. At the age of 55, Rimsky-Korsakov wrote to a lady friend who, in her letter, wished him to spend the coming weekend in an A-major mood:

> You wish me an A major mood. Well, let me tell you that the key of E-flat major is quite good enough for me! A major is not fitting for a man of my age. A major is the key of youth and spring . . . not the spring when the puddles are still covered with ice, but the spring when lilacs are blooming and all the meadows are covered with flowers. A major is the key of dawn— not when the light is just breaking, but a bit later, when the East is all crimson and gold!

It is evident that Rimsky-Korsakov's feelings for this key are not much different from Mozart's or Puccini's.

There is an even more general agreement regarding the meaning of the key of F minor. It seems that this key has a remarkable affinity for weeping. I made a list of compositions featuring F-minor tears and sobs. It begins with Bach and Handel and includes examples by Mozart, Schubert, Donizetti, Wagner, Puccini, and more than a dozen other well-known composers. In the opening scene of *Forza*, Leonora sobs in F minor at the thought of leaving her father and her country [80]. F-minor tears can also be agitated and rapid, as when Leonora pleads with Father Guardiano to allow her to enter the convent [81].

You can see that there is a rather surprising consensus regarding certain keys. Let us now turn to what I call the long-range reasons for choosing certain keys. In the shaping of an opera one of the most important aims is the creation of contrasts—contrasts between different characters and also contrasts in the feelings of the same character. Here a composer can be greatly helped by the difference between keys having sharps and those with flats. The key of C major, which has neither sharps nor flats, is thought of as lying at the dead center of the whole system of keys. In one direction from C major, up the circle of fifths, are the keys with sharps: G major with one sharp, D major with two sharps, and so on. In the opposite direction from C major, down the circle of fifths, are the flats: F major, B-flat major, E-flat major, and so forth. Neighboring keys are related to each other, but those that are far apart can be juxtaposed for contrast.

Let us see how this idea of contrasting keys works in *La Forza del Destino*. At the root of the tragedy is the Spanish pride and honor of the Marquis of Calatrava and his contemptuous rejection of Don Alvaro, whom he regards as an unworthy and low-class alien. As far as Verdi was concerned, the old Marquis has four sharps in his coat of arms. He is an immovable character who lives and dies in E major and in C-sharp minor, both of which have four sharps. The exotic and romantic Alvaro, who has royal Inca blood in his veins, is an absolute contrast to the family of the Calatravas. Alvaro's native land is half a world away from Spain. His is the country of flat keys. I do not know of any other operatic character who does so much singing in A-flat minor, the key with seven flats.

In the love duet near the end of the first act, Leonora promises to follow Alvaro "a gl'ultimi confini della terra" ("to the farthest ends of the world") [82], and the key of this duet—G-flat major, with its six flats—

is truly at the end of the world from her family's native E major. Her brother, Don Carlo, inherits his father's E-major characteristics, and the contrast between him and Alvaro is maintained throughout the opera.

In the confrontation between the two men in the last act, Carlo sings in his proud and insolent E major, with four sharps [83], while Alvaro has his seven flats [84]. Even when Don Carlo has to hide his identity, he moves over only one sharp, to the neighboring key of A major, with three sharps. At the first meeting of Carlo and Alvaro, they introduce themselves to each other under false names and in slightly disguised keys. "I am Don Felice de Bornos, Adjutant to the General," says Carlo in A major:

Don Fe-li - ce de Bor-nos   a-iu-tan - te del   du - ce...

"And I am Captain of the Grenadiers Don Federico Herreras," answers Alvaro masquerading in D-flat major, with only five flats:

Io   ca - pi - tan de' Gran-a - tie - ri   Don Fe-de - ri - co Her-re - ros.

All this seems to be completely consistent and logical, but if you ask me whether Verdi chose all these keys on purpose, in a fully conscious calculation of what he was doing, I must admit that I don't think so. The very fact that he originally set Don Carlo's longest and most important aria in F major, a key with one flat, shows that he did not necessarily think of Carlo as an E-major character. But, as I mentioned earlier, the aria did not remain in F major. It was Don Carlo's inheritance and fate to be an E-major person. He just was not comfortable in a key with one flat in it. And little by little even Verdi had to give in, and let Don Carlo have his way. Such is the logic of keys.

Perhaps we should call it "La Forza del Destino Musicale"—"The Power of Musical Destiny"!

LA GIOCONDA

by Amilcare Ponchielli

The action of La Gioconda *takes place in Venice in the seventeenth century. A banished Genoese nobleman, Enzo Grimaldo, is loved by both the street singer La Gioconda and Laura, the wife of the Venetian government official Alvise. When the amorous advances of the Inquisition spy Barnaba are repulsed by La Gioconda, he denounces her blind mother (La Cieca) as a witch. Alvise has La Cieca arrested, but Laura obtains mercy for her, and La Cieca gives her a rosary in gratitude. Laura recognizes Enzo, and so does Barnaba, who promises Enzo that he will help him run away with Laura. Barnaba then denounces Laura's unfaithfulness in a letter. La Gioconda is horrified to overhear it being dictated. In the second act, Barnaba guides Laura to the island where Enzo's boat is anchored. La Gioconda appears and is about to stab her rival when she recognizes Laura's rosary.*

In the third act Alvise accuses his wife of infidelity, but the poison she is ordered to drink is changed into a sleeping potion by La Gioconda. At a party later the same evening, Barnaba finds La Cieca praying for the dead. Alvise reveals his wife's body to his guests. Enzo attacks him but is hauled off to prison along with the blind woman. La Gioconda offers herself to Barnaba if he will rescue Enzo. In the last act, the unconscious Laura is carried to the island of Giudecca. Enzo appears and is reunited with Laura, who has awakened from her sleep, and they escape. When Barnaba arrives to claim his reward, La Gioconda stabs herself. The enraged Barnaba shouts at La Gioconda that he has killed her mother.

Broadcast January 17, 1981   Cassette illustrations 85–91

T HE TITLE OF *La Gioconda* is taken from the name of its leading female character. Early in the first act, the soprano identifies herself with the words "Mi chiaman La Gioconda" ("They call me the Cheerful One, for I sing my happy songs to the whole world"). Considering what happens to her later, calling her "the Cheerful One" is, I'm afraid, the height of irony. Some seventy years ago, Henry Krehbiel, one of New York's most distinguished music critics, suggested that a more appropriate name for the heroine would be "La Dolorosa" ("the Suffering One"). As the plot progresses, we might feel like calling her "the Vengeful One," and later on, "the Self-Sacrificing One." But probably the best appellation of all would be "La Sfortunata" ("the Unfortunate One"). Both the *dolorosa* and the *sfortunata* aspects of La Gioconda are expressed with moving eloquence by the leading soprano herself in the final moments of the first act. "Il mio destino e questo, o morte o amor!" ("It is my destiny to hover between love and death") [85]. The very last word she sings in the first act is *dolor* ("sorrow")!

Gioconda's misfortunes begin early in the first act, when she rejects the amorous advances of the infamous spy Barnaba. In order to win her, he starts fashioning devilish intrigues, which lead to a succession of criminal events of quite unusual ferocity, even by operatic standards. *La Gioconda* was written more than a century ago, and during these hundred years we have certainly been exposed to countless examples of operatic violence. Think of the shocking events in *Lulu* or in *The Dialogues of the Carmelites*. Add, if you will, the four victims of brutality in Puccini's *Tosca*. I would not be surprised if the gory events in *La Gioconda* outstrip all these put together.

A catalogue of evil deeds in this opera could begin with three attempted murders: In the first act a mob of superstitious sailors accuses Gioconda's blind mother of being a witch and is about to burn her at the stake. In the second act, Alvise, the outraged husband, is unable to kill Laura, his unfaithful wife, with his dagger, so on the following evening he tries to force her to drink poison. Finally, in the fourth act, Enzo is ready to plunge his sword into the heart of his former sweetheart, Gioconda. While these attempts are thwarted by last-minute interventions, the opera can still boast—if boast is the right word—of at least one murder and one suicide, each of which is allowed to run its prescribed course.

The plot abounds in other spectacular deeds of villainy: blackmail, denunciations, false accusations, and double dealings. To enliven this parade of criminal activities, the story also features a folk dance in the first act; the burning of a ship in full view of the audience in the second act; an extended formal ballet in the third act; and the robbing of a grave during the last intermission. This aggregation of lurid happenings has led many connoisseurs of opera to reject *La Gioconda* as a worthless and vulgar melodrama.

The truth of the matter is that the opera is a spectacular example of a story wherein larger-than-life characters give vent to their frenzied passions through the medium of larger-than-life music. Nor is this so very unusual in the realm of opera. When all is said and done, Tristan and Isolde also express their frenzied passions by means of larger-than-life music. With Wagner much of the frenzy is allocated to the orchestra, while in *Gioconda* all the passions originate, flourish, and expand in the vocal line.

Instead of dealing with Schopenhauer's metaphysical concepts of the Day and the Night, the emotions in Boïto's libretto are couched in much less philosophical terms. For instance, in the duet between Laura and Gioconda in the second act, the two women argue about the relative strength of their love for Enzo. Gioconda declares that she adores him "as the lion craves blood; as the whirlwind enjoys its flight; as the lightning loves the clouds; as the kingfisher welcomes the plunge into the abyss; as the eagle worships the sun." We may smile at Gioconda's choice of similes, but we must admire the magnificence of her vocal line. It moves in majestic curves across two full octaves, from a low C flat to a high C flat [86].

This is Italian vocalization at its most gorgeous, but the soprano is by no means the only one whose passionate utterances travel over the entire extent of the singer's emotional and vocal range. Each of the other five leading characters, in solo numbers or in ensemble pieces, gives vent to similar uninhibited outbursts of emotion clothed in larger-than-life vocalism. In the first act Gioconda's blind mother, La Cieca, hands her rosary to Laura, who had interceded for her, and invokes her blessing on Laura's head. La Cieca's vocal line oscillates between the high G and the low B flat of the contralto's range [87]. Only the most accomplished singers can navigate these perilous waters and do justice to the overwhelming vocal demands of Ponchielli's score.

The three leading men in *La Gioconda* are as singlemindedly obsessed as the women. Laura's husband, Alvise—one of the heads of the Venetian government—is somewhat less complicated a character than the other two men. He does not get to sing much in the first act, but clearly at that point he still feels some love or at least respect for his wife, since he grants her request to set La Cieca free. But after learning of Laura's infidelity, he does not hesitate to avenge himself in the time-honored manner by sentencing his guilty wife to death and openly claiming credit for having done so. Barnaba, who is probably the most infamous villain in the entire operatic repertoire, is an even more colorful character. Being the chief spy in the service of the Venetian Inquisition makes him all-powerful. But he prefers to stalk his prey while masquerading as an innocent-looking, guitar-strumming minstrel or as a carefree fisherman. In this second disguise, he sings a very curious ditty that manages to combine the lilt of a Venetian gondolier's tune with the wicked accents of an out-and-out double-crosser. At least this is the effect this song has always had on me [88].

In his lecherous lusting for Gioconda, who cannot stand the sight of him, Barnaba stops at nothing. Knowing that her mother and Enzo are the only two creatures in the world whom Gioconda loves, Barnaba does his utmost to get both of them under his thumb. When, in the first act, the mother accidentally escapes his clutches, Barnaba concentrates his efforts on Enzo. And, by the end of the third act, he achieves his goal. Enzo is in his power, and Gioconda promises to submit to Barnaba in exchange for Enzo's freedom. Opera-lovers who complain that these stratagems are too blatantly melodramatic should consider that they accept the validity of the identical type of blackmail in Puccini's *Tosca*. The main difference is that when Scarpia is ready to claim his reward, Tosca kills him; while Gioconda—who knows that by this time Enzo is safe—kills herself. I find both solutions equally believable.

In the last scene of the opera, Gioconda finally gets a chance to demonstrate the "cheerful" songs that, as she claims in the first act, are her specialty. This last duet—during which Gioconda vocalizes happily, as she looks for the dagger while adorning herself for Barnaba, and he gloats, believing that he is about to reach his goal—is one of the most chilling and morbid episodes in all Italian opera [89].

When it comes to Enzo, I must confess that my feelings are rather ambivalent. In the first act, Barnaba, who seems to be completely informed of every detail of Enzo's life, states that Enzo loved Gioconda as a brother while he loved Laura as a lover. And it is true that from the moment Enzo realizes there is a chance that Laura will leave her husband and run away with him, he becomes completely obsessed with this possibility. Even though he has sworn eternal fidelity to Gioconda, Enzo seems quite willing to break her heart, hoping only that by losing him she will not suffer *too* much! Romantic heroes are not supposed to behave in this fashion even if they are in the throes of obsessive love. There is no doubt, incidentally, that Gioconda thinks of Enzo as her lover, and it seems rather unfair that Alvise's unfaithful wife and Gioconda's unfaithful lover should be permitted to escape all punishment and presumably live happily ever after. In spite of Enzo's shockingly callous treatment of Gioconda, I must admit that where Laura is concerned he is capable of the most appealing tenderness. I am particularly fond of the phrases Enzo sings in the second act, just before the well-known moonrise duet. Accompanied by woodwinds, this short solo sequence, in which Enzo allays Laura's fears, is perhaps the most touching episode in the entire opera [90].

Finally, while it is true that the arias and big spectacle scenes are the most famous sections of *La Gioconda*, there is at least one quiet ensemble piece for three voices that is very much worth looking forward to. The Farewell Trio of the fourth act, in which Gioconda asks the escaping lovers not to forget her, can take its place next to the best Verdi ever produced in this line [91].

HANSEL AND GRETEL

By Engelbert Humperdinck

Broadcast December 27, 1980   Cassette illustrations 92–109

T HE GENESIS OF Humperdinck's *Hansel and Gretel* is, in itself, a sort of Christmas fairy tale. Humperdinck's sister, Adelheid Wette, was in the habit of concocting little playlets to be acted by her two teen-age daughters. On one occasion, she asked her brother—who was then 36 years old and had not produced anything of particular importance—to compose a dance for a skit based on a Grimm fairy tale. The tune he wrote was "Brüderchen, komm tanz' mit mir, Beide Händchen reich' ich dir" [92]. The girls were delighted and wanted more. One thing led to another. The musical fairy tale kept growing and growing until it became the wonderful full-fledged opera we hear today. There have been many operas written for children and about children, but *Hansel and Gretel* is the only one that has stood the test of time. It is now 87 years old, and I am convinced that it will be just as popular when it celebrates its 200th birthday.

The opera's longevity is not surprising, for *Hansel and Gretel* offers listeners and viewers a very unusual and probably unique blend of simplicity and sophistication. On the one hand, the composer has given us dozens of delightfully tuneful melodies. But we are also exposed to dramatic episodes of the most impressive orchestral and musical complication. To stress the fairy-tale aspect of his opera, Humperdinck starts each of its three scenes with authentic German folktunes. At the beginning the children sing about barefoot geese that need no shoes, and of the way to get rid of fleabites by sleeping in the straw [93]. In the second scene, in the Forest, Gretel hums a genuine German riddle-song describing a little mannikin who stands all alone in the woods:

He has a red mantle around him and a black cap on his head. I had always thought that the solution to the riddle was "a mushroom," but recently I read that the German answer was *die Hagebutte* ("the rose hip"). Act 2 opens with the third of the opera's authentic folksongs, the German "Ringel, ringel, reihe," which our children know as "Ring around the rosy":

Humperdinck's sister changed the original idea into a question-and-answer dialogue, which is heard later in the same scene, and with the same tune, when the witch asks, "Nibble, nibble Mousey, who's nibbling at my housey?"

The children answer, "The wind, the wind, the heavenly wind" [94].

There are at least eight or nine other charming short melodies in the opera that could just as easily belong to that anonymous treasure trove known as folk music. In the first act, in addition to the polka-like dance tune about the geese, there is the refrain of the father's monologue, when he brings home the big basket of food [95]. The "Go to sleep" song of the first Forest Scene, when the magic sand is thrown into the children's eyes is another:

This tune, in a faster tempo, reappears at the beginning of the second act, when the Dawn Fairy appears with a large bluebell and shakes drops of glockenspiel dew into the eyes of the sleeping children [96]. The final episode with the witch features several more folk-like tunes, such as the "gingerbread house" phrase [97] and the invitation tune, "Come little mousey, come into my housey" [98]. Two more are heard as the magic spell stiffens the children into immobility [99] and as the reverse of the same phrase [100] breaks the spell and unlocks their joints and muscles. All these, as well as several other melodies in the opera, have that special unforgettable quality that we normally associate with simple folk music.

What is more startling is what occurs in the orchestra pit, where the music is replete with involved elaborations of single melodies and the most refined combinations of several different tunes. These orchestral complications are not really surprising when one considers that Engelbert Humperdinck was a devoted disciple of Richard Wagner, whose orchestral textures—in his later works—consist almost entirely of interweaving of significant thematic material.

Wagner met Humperdinck in Italy and took him to Bayreuth, where he made the young musician copy the orchestral score of *Parsifal*. This was a wonderful training exercise for Humperdinck, who later confessed that he learned more about orchestration and composition in several weeks with Wagner than he could have accomplished in several years of regular conservatory studies. During the final rehearsals for the *Parsifal* première, in the summer of 1882, Humperdinck not only took charge of the children's choruses in *Parsifal* but was also privileged to add a few measures of his own to the first act of Wagner's opera.

Wagner had specified that the transition between the two scenes of the first act of *Parsifal* be effected without lowering the main curtain. Instead, the background drops of the forest scenery were supposed to unroll slowly in full view of the audience, gradually changing the forest into a walled passage and then into the colonnaded temple of the knights of the Holy Grail. During this time, Parsifal and Gurnemanz had to pretend to walk while actually remaining in place. This was meant to illustrate the philosophic principle enunciated by Gurnemanz with the words, "Zum Raum wird hier die Zeit" ("Here time turns into space")—a startling anticipation of Einstein's theory of relativity.

The trouble was that the space-time continuum imagined by Wagner and the movement of the machinery constructed by Wagner's engineers did not jibe. Wagner's transformation music lasts approximately $3\frac{1}{2}$ minutes, but at the first run-through of this episode it was discovered that the unrolling of the scenery took more than twice that long. The only solution was to play the music twice. That, unfortunately, presented another problem. Wagner's transformation passage begins in D-flat major:

But it ends half a tone lower, in C major:

That made a simple repetition impossible.

Wagner became so incensed with the whole mix-up that he refused to have anything to do with it. It was young Humperdinck who saved the day by composing a bridge passage that connected the C-major ending to the second entrance of the D-flat major phrase. Much to the young assistant's joy, Wagner accepted his contribution, and at the 1882 première of *Parsifal* the audience heard several measures of music that were Humperdinck's rather than Wagner's. Later, the machinery was speeded up, and Humperdinck's bridge passage became unnecessary.

However, Wagner's musical procedures were not forgotten by his one-time assistant. There are several episodes in *Hansel and Gretel* in which Humperdinck's orchestra succeeds in out-Wagnering Wagner. It is done so cleverly that the audience's attention is never deflected from the exciting stage events. But a man of my type, who likes to listen to music in slow motion and to study orchestral scores with a magnifying glass, finds a careful analysis very rewarding.

In the second scene, as darkness falls and the children are preparing to return home, Hansel looks first in one direction, then in another, and finally confesses, "Gretel, I cannot find the way. I think we're really lost":

Following this announcement, Gretel becomes progressively more and more scared. Hansel tries to reassure her, but she is convinced that strange creatures are waving their hands and making faces at her. When the fireflies appear, she becomes downright hysterical.

To translate Gretel's gradually growing fear into orchestral terms, Humperdinck introduces a special theme—I like to call it the "I am frightened" theme. To stress its importance, the composer entrusts it to the English horn, an orchestral instrument that had not been heard previously in the opera. The first four notes of this phrase become a separate motif that is repeated and elaborated in a most spectacular manner. At first the theme is presented slowly, like a car that travels in first gear:

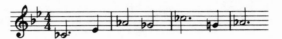

But very soon, the speed is doubled:

and in this second-gear tempo, the phrase is made to travel from one orchestral instrument to another:

from the cellos to the bassoons and the clarinets [101], then again to the double basses, cellos, and French horns [102]. As Gretel imagines that the tree stump is making faces at her, the speed of the motif doubles again, moving, as it were, into third gear. It is now combined with barking noises in the French horns, bassoons, and clarinets:

When the fireflies appear along with other blinking and flashing lights, a new theme—related to the witch's ride music—makes its appearance in the piccolos and flutes [103]. It does not appear alone, however, but is immediately combined with the trombones, which intone the

"I'm frightened" phrase in first gear {104}. Soon thereafter the second- and third-gear themes are combined:

and, at the same time, the firefly phrases are added:

Later, the "I'm frightened" theme makes a still more unusual appearance in the bass clarinet, an instrument that has been kept in reserve for this very purpose {105}. Humperdinck's orchestral resources are by no means exhausted even now. Before the Sandman comes to calm the children, the "I'm frightened" theme actually speeds up even more, moving it into a fourth gear {106}.

You can take my word for it that much of this orchestral accompaniment cannot be played adequately on the piano. Fortunately, there are not too many such finger-breaking episodes in the opera. Perhaps the most wicked section, from the pianist's point of view, is the Waltz played by the orchestra near the end of the opera, after the witch is pushed into the oven. Here, three different themes are introduced at one and the same time:

On one occasion I was forced to play a section of today's opera some twenty times in a row—not just to practice it at home, but in public, if you please! Many years ago I toured with a miniature, children's version of *Hansel and Gretel*. We used only three singers: Gretel, Hansel, and the witch, but we had nice settings and costumes. I accompanied the show on the piano, and the whole thing was quite a successful undertaking. We also had a very clever stage carpenter, who rigged up a contraption that made it look as if our witch were actually flying. A large doll, sitting on a broom, and dressed exactly like our singer, was released from the wings at the proper time. It glided over the roof of the gingerbread house and disappeared on the opposite side of the stage. At the end of her song with the broomstick, our singing witch would dance off into the right wing and then run across the stage behind the sky drop, so that at the end of the instrumental interlude, she could emerge from the opposite side and sing her final "Prrr, Broomstick hold!"

Many of the little children in the audience were taken in by this trick and actually believed that our singing witch could fly on her broomstick. On one of these tours, we played at the high school in Keene, New Hampshire. It was an afternoon show and everything was going well. The witch danced, sang her multiplication-table song [107], and galloped off into the right wing. The doll flew over the gingerbread house, and I played the interlude music as usual [108]. But when I came to the end of the interlude, the witch did not reappear. Figuring that something must have delayed her for a few seconds, I went back and repeated the last eight measures. Again, there was no witch. So, I played it over, but still no witch! I was completely baffled. I had seen her dancing off to the right, and we always checked the space behind the skydrop to make sure that she could cross over. Even if she could not do so, I thought, she certainly would have returned from the same wing into which she had disappeared. I kept playing and playing. Eventually, after I had repeated those eight measures 20 or 25 times—I lost count—she did reappear from the left wing, somewhat out of breath, sang her "Prrr, Broomstick, hold!" [109], and the show continued smoothly.

After the performance I ran backstage to find out what had happened. "For goodness sake, Eunice," I asked. "Where were you all that time?" "You won't believe it, Mr. G." she said. "When I danced off into the right wing, it was quite dark there. Looking for the passage across, I opened a door and found myself in the school yard. The door closed and locked behind me. I pounded, but no one heard me!" "For Pete's sake," I said. "What did you do?" "What could I do? I ran around the school building as fast as my legs would take me, dashed through the main entrance, and managed somehow to find my way backstage." "You ran around the school in plain daylight, dressed as a witch, with a broom in your hand?" I asked. "That's right," she said!

When you hear this music, *do* think of me playing it over and over again, while the witch was running around the school in Keene, New Hampshire.

IDOMENEO

by Wolfgang Amadeus Mozart

Broadcast January 15, 1983   Cassette illustrations 110–124

M OZART, WHOSE operatic music invariably illuminates the subtlest nuances of human behavior, was seemingly not particularly sensitive to the beauties of nature. This is especially noticeable in his lack of interest in the activities of the winds and waves of the open sea. There *is* of course the delicious Terzettino in the first act of *Così fan tutte*, in which the softly murmuring muted violins imitate the gentle movement of the waves:

This is the only "water music" in the seven famous operas Mozart composed in the last ten years of his life.

How different this is from the task facing Mozart when, at the age of 24, he was commissioned to write *Idomeneo*! He had to create a musical framework for a story that takes place on a land surrounded by water and in which all the events are motivated by the storms and other angry manifestations of the god of the sea. This turbulent atmosphere is evident not only in the actual tempests but also in episodes in which anxieties and fears felt by individual characters create upheavals no less violent than those attributable directly to the wrath of Neptune. In the midst of all these storms and stresses, there is only one scene in which the sea is calm. In the middle of the second act—when Electra is preparing for her trip to Greece—the choristers, with gently lilting accents, praise the smoothness of the sea: "Placido è il mar" [110]. Even Electra forgets her erstwhile jealousy and anticipates a voyage with her beloved Idamante by singing the most graceful and liquid strains [111]. This lovely scene, dealing with soft zephyrs and smooth waters, is one of the few relaxed episodes of the opera, which is dominated by the anger and rage of Neptune.

The tumultuous sea storms of the first two acts are so realistically depicted in the orchestra that one wonders where Mozart could have acquired firsthand knowledge of such violent phenomena. There were only two occasions when he took part in a sea voyage. He crossed the English channel when he was eight years old, and returned from England the same way a year later. For the trip over, his father hired a small barge in order to save money. They sailed in the month of April, when the sea was unusually rough, and the passengers suffered mightily from seasickness. It was then that young Mozart was exposed to the rolling of waves crowned with white caps, the sudden gusts and the howling of the wind, the splashing of the foam, and the roar of the ground swell, all of which are so magnificently embodied in the music of *Idomeneo*.

The first storm of the opera occurs in the Overture. I imagine that it was during this cataclysm that the ship transporting the Trojan Princess Ilia and other Trojan captives was sent to the bottom of the sea. A few of the drowning prisoners of war were rescued, but most important of all, Ilia—as she recounts in her opening aria—was lifted from the waves by King Idomeneo's son, Idamante. The fury of Neptune is evident in the whirling crescendos of the strings and the angry groans of the French horns [112]. The first meeting of the young people, destined to love each other, is heard in the second theme of the Overture [113]. In the opening scene, Idamante admits his adoration openly, in front of everyone. But Ilia, again in her first aria, is conscience-stricken that she—the daughter of the Trojan King Priam—should have fallen in love with a man whose father was responsible for the death of her entire family. "My duty bids me hate him," she sings [114]. But this is followed immediately by a most touching and eloquent confession: "Yet now that I've seen him, oh, heaven, my heart belongs to him alone!" [115].

This romantic involvement is the rather unexpected result of the first storm! The second storm breaks out after the counsellor, Arbace, announces the probable demise of King Idomeneo, whose ship has been seen foundering near the shore of the island. This upheaval coincides with the emotional distress of the haughty Princess Electra, who is not a stranger to present-day opera lovers familiar with Richard Strauss's opera bearing her name. It would appear that after Electra helped her brother, Orestes, kill their mother, Clytemnestra, she was forced to leave her native Argos and take refuge on the island of Crete. Since the crime of matricide, regardless of the provocation, was not forgivable in Greek mythology, Electra will be haunted forever by the memories of her murderous deed.

At this moment, however, Electra is in the throes of other emotions, those of jealousy and hatred. Having fallen in love with Idamante and re-alizing that he prefers Princess Ilia, she is filled with foreboding at the announcement of King Idomeneo's probable death. She has no doubt that once Idamante becomes king of Crete, nothing and no one will be able to prevent him from taking Ilia for his wife. In Electra's aria, Mozart creates a most unusual amalgam of two types of storms, those of natural and those of human origin. First, there is the turbulence of the wind, as it gradually gathers force [116]. Then, to emphasize the kinship between the turmoil of nature and Electra's growing frenzy, Mozart fashions a star-tling musical concept. Interrupting the sequence of regular, *alla-breve* progressions, he injects a completely unexpected succession of explosive triple-time phrases [117].

Next, we are introduced to the frightening images that are taking possession of Electra's distracted mind—"I feel the furies of the under-world invading my bosom!" [118]. At the end of her aria, the conjunction of the incompatible double- and triple-time rhythmic elements gathers force to produce an overwhelming effect, as if the whole fabric of musical time and space is being torn to shreds [119]. This leads us to the shore, where the arpeggios of the strings, interspersed with wildly crisscrossing scales and daggerlike flashes of sixteenth notes, give a graphic musical representation of the relentless assault of the waves [120]. Equally impres-sive are the antiphonal exchanges between the two male choral groups: the calls for help of the drowning Cretan soldiers, which are answered by the laments of the islanders, praying to Neptune for mercy [121].

During this period of violent upheaval and lamentation, Idomeneo makes a solemn oath that if he survives the storm, he will sacrifice to Nep-tune the first human being he meets on shore. Ten years earlier, when the Cretans went to war, their fleet numbered 80 ships. Having foolishly pro-voked Neptune's wrath after the conquest of Troy, Idomeneo is now faced with the prospect of losing all his remaining ships. No wonder he is will-ing to do anything to mollify the god's anger! Since the first person Ido-

meneo meets on shore is his son and only child, Idamante, the oath becomes the crux and mainspring of the action. A similar vow promising
a human sacrifice occurs in the Bible, in the Book of Judges, when
Jephthah is forced to disown and punish his daughter and only child.
There is, however, an important difference: Jephthah, though broken-
hearted, does not for a moment consider the possibility of breaking *his*
vow; while Idomeneo desperately tries to find some means of saving the
life of *his* only child.

In consultation with his friend and advisor, Arbace, Idomeneo hopes
to avoid sacrificing his son by removing Idamante from Crete: Idamante
will escort Princess Electra to her native Argos. The notion of saving Idamante's life while exposing him to the dangers of a sea voyage, where he
would be completely at the mercy of Neptune, may seem naive and illogical. But it is not Idamante's life that is at issue here, but rather the moral
fiber and trustworthiness of Idomeneo. The so-called Serious Operas—of
which *Idomeneo* is a leading example—were not, like Mozart's other operas, written for the entertainment of theatrical audiences. They were
meant to be performed at imperial and ducal courts and were designed for
the education and edification of princes and princesses. The lesson they
taught was that *obedience was all-important*. Children had to obey their parents. Kings and heroes had to obey gods and goddesses. We listen with
compassion as Idomeneo compares his tragic situation with the storms of
the sea, and we admire Mozart's skill in describing emotional anxieties in
terms resembling the fluctuations of turbulent waters [122]. But nevertheless a king who breaks his solemn oath to a deity is not fit to be a king.
And that is the point of the sudden, overwhelming catastrophe that
strikes the Cretan harbor at the end of the second act.

From the musical point of view this third storm is truly gigantic. In
my opinion it is more inventive and more frightening than the tempests
in Gluck's *Iphigenia in Tauris*, Verdi's *Rigoletto* and *Otello*, or Wagner's *Die
Walküre*. It is an orchestral and choral storm with a startling and totally
unexpected change of key. After several passages in C minor:

we are suddenly plunged into an extended B-flat minor sequence {123}. The unprepared juxtaposition of these two keys:

is without parallel in music. You cannot even call it "modern music"; it is simply unique.

In the final section of this number, the chorus sings "Corriamo, fuggiamo" ("Let us run, let us flee!"), and before the choristers actually leave the stage, they repeat these words almost a hundred times! Some listeners find these endless repetitions hard to take. "For heaven's sake," they say. "If you want to run and flee, why don't you do it?" But the Cretans *do* run and they *do* try to flee. But no matter which direction they turn—right, left, toward the sea, or away from it—they encounter thunder and lightnings, cataracts of rain, black clouds, and other dreadful signs of Neptune's anger. I am afraid that some day, when we get punished by the wrath of God, we will also keep saying "Let us flee," and there will be no way to escape {124}!

Be that as it may, Idomeneo's defiance of the laws of heaven endangers his kingdom, and he must therefore be relieved of his kingship. Ilia's and Idamante's willingness to accept the decree of Neptune makes them worthy to become the next rulers of Crete. And, after the oracle announces this decision of heaven, the final chorus celebrates a happy ending. But before that can occur, Mozart regales us with another tempestuous episode, which embodies what are perhaps the most ferocious expressions of insane rage in the entire operatic literature.

"Oh, agony; oh, torture," Electra sings, as she realizes the full import of the oracle's decision. "Will I see Idamante in the arms of my rival?" she asks, while a convulsive tremor shakes her entire being. This phrase ends on a soft F-major chord:

Then something dreadful happens: supported by loud trumpets and kettle-drums, a totally irrational D-major explosion takes place:

I say "irrational" because musically speaking this unprepared D-major fanfare makes no sense. And more important, at this moment Electra goes insane. Her final aria is a most fitting climax to the many storms in this extraordinary opera, conceived and executed in less than five months by a 24-year-old youth.

We must keep in mind that *Idomeneo* is number 366 in Köchel's complete catalog of Mozart's compositions. That means that before starting to compose this opera, Mozart had completed 365 other works, including many symphonies, concertos, and no fewer than ten other operas. We must be grateful that we live on a planet where such miracles are possible!

JENÚFA

by Leoš Janáček

In a mill town in the Moravian mountains live the ne'er-do-well Števa; his half brother, Laca, a farmhand; and their cousin Jenúfa (foster daughter of the proud and imperious Kostelnička), who helps in the house. Jenúfa is expecting Števa's child and anxiously awaiting the result of a military conscription ballot to know whether Števa will be free to marry her. When Števa turns up unrecruited but drunk, Kostelnička forbids him to marry Jenúfa until he has proved his worth by a year's total abstinence from liquor. After Števa leaves, Laca offers Jenúfa flowers and tries to kiss her. When she repels him, he slashes her face with a knife. Several months later, Jenúfa secretly gives birth to a son. Kostelnička, tormented by the disgrace, sends for Števa to marry Jenúfa, but he refuses and denies all responsibility. Laca appears, penitent and willing to marry Jenúfa though shocked at hearing of the birth of Števa's child. Hoping to help matters along, Kostelnička tells Laca that the child has died, and then, unbeknownst to Jenúfa, she drowns the baby in a brook. During the marriage ceremony between Jenúfa and Laca, word comes that the body of a newborn infant has been found under the ice. To save Jenúfa from being accused of murder, Kostelnička steps forward and confesses her guilt. As Kostelnička is being led away, Jenúfa offers Laca his freedom, but he is faithful and pledges his love.

Broadcast December 21, 1974   Cassette illustrations 125–141

Opera-lovers hearing Janáček's *Jenúfa* for the first time will find much that is familiar to them and also much that is new and startling, both in the story and in the music. What happens in the first act—the troubles of a pregnant girl whose prospects of speedy marriage are vanishing and who, on top of that, has to defend herself against the violent advances of an unwelcome suitor—reminds us very strongly of the operatic village life as we know it from Mascagni's *Cavalleria Rusticana* and Leoncavallo's *Pagliacci*. Jenúfa's pleading with Števa is not very different from Santuzza's tearful appeal to Turiddu; and Laca's violence, which erupts so explosively and unfortunately just before the curtain falls on the first act, is strongly reminiscent of Tonio's attempted attack on Nedda.

But in the second act, something quite unexpected develops. For one thing, a dramatic personage who appears for only a few minutes in the first act turns out to be the prime mover in the tragic events that are about to unfold. As a matter of fact, the play on which the opera is based was not called *Jenúfa*. Its original title was *Její Pastorkyňa* ("Her Foster Daughter"), and that was also the original title of the opera. Kostelnička, the foster mother—an angry, older woman—puts a halt to the riotous singing and dancing in the first act and lays down the law that Jenúfa's marriage must be delayed for one year, during which time Jenúfa's sweetheart, Števa, must behave himself and remain sober.

Jenúfa's disgrace—giving birth to an illegitimate child—is a particularly terrible blow to her foster mother, who is recognized in the village as the authority and last word in all matters pertaining to morality. Her very title, Kostelnička, comes from the word *kostel*, meaning "church"; it can be translated as "sacristan's" or "church sexton's widow" and indicates her special position among the villagers.

Kostelnička's haughty presumption of moral authority is surpassed only by her pride in her foster daughter, Jenúfa; not only because of Jenufa's beauty and popularity but also because of her superior mind. A short episode near the beginning of the first act involving the shepherd boy Jano was included to show us that Jenúfa is smart enough to teach the peasant boys and girls how to read and write; that she, in Grandmother Burja's words, "has a man's common sense like her foster mother." "There is no doubt," the old grandmother says, "that Jenúfa should have been a schoolteacher."

But now the disgraceful situation of the formerly level-headed and chaste Jenúfa has shaken her foster mother's self-respect to its very foundations. Kostelnička's wounded pride and her resulting emotional anguish are shown very tellingly in one of the most eloquent vocal and musical episodes of the opera. Near the beginning of the second act she reveals her deep humiliation to Jenúfa: "I was so proud! Oh, how proud I was of you!" {125}. This sentence is repeated over and over again by Kostelnička, and even after the vocal portion is over, the full orchestra continues to elaborate on this theme, repeating it another half-dozen times {126}. The composer obviously wanted to make sure that his listeners were fully aware of this tune, which is psychologically and musically at the very center of the drama.

In the second act one can see in minute detail the gradual emotional, mental, and moral collapse of the church sexton's widow. Kostelnička's wounded pride and her desperate need to save her foster daughter's and her own reputation eventually drive her to the ultimate solution—murdering Jenúfa's baby. It is truly astonishing to what extent this newborn child, hidden in Jenúfa's room offstage, influences and dominates all the events of the second act. Even before the curtain rises—during the orchestral introduction—there is a graphic musical picture of the tragic situation confronting Kostelnička. The drum beats:

obviously portray Kostelnička's shock when she discovers Jenúfa's pregnancy. They are followed by a gloomy, restless passage depicting the mental anguish of those twenty weeks of waiting for the child to be born {127}. During those weeks, with the shutters closed to keep the neighbors from discovering Jenúfa's presence, Kostelnička prays and fasts, and prays again, asking God that the child might be stillborn {128}. And then comes another shock, when a strong, healthy child is born {129}.

The question arises, "What to do now?" The last four notes of this phrase:

become a nagging obsession in Kostelnička's vocal lines as well as in the orchestra. "When you told me—when you confessed to me":

is always punctuated by the orchestra:

When Kostelnička sings, "Then I thought such disgrace would kill me!"

this four-note phrase also gets connected with her contempt and hatred of
Števa. "And all this time the baby's father—that worthy fellow—did not
care a rap!"

In the next episode Jenúfa gazes affectionately at the baby's crib offstage, and the music portrays her love and tenderness [130]. But the obsessive refrain of her foster mother's despair and hatred continues to inter-
fere with Jenúfa's maternal tenderness. For Kostelnička is still hoping for
the child's death: "Pray that God will take him from you!" [131]. But
since the week-old baby is obviously strong and healthy and is the very
image of his father, the only thing to do, Kostelnička feels, is to persuade
Števa to do the decent thing: admit the paternity of the child and marry
the girl.

Having sent an urgent note to Števa, Kostelnička gives a sleeping
potion to Jenúfa to keep her from interfering. Kostelnička is now ready
for the distasteful chore of facing that unworthy spoiled brat of a father.
The formerly imperious and autocratic Kostelnička demeans herself and
finally goes down on her knees, pleading with her nephew to accept the
child and make an honest woman of Jenúfa. This scene, I believe, is one of
the most pathetic in all operatic literature. After the reluctant Števa is
induced to look at his baby son, he has a momentary feeling of compassion. "Poor little mite," he says. But his selfishness comes out imme-

diately in the sentence: "I will gladly support him. But it must not be known that I'm the father!"

"But what of Jenúfa?" Kostelnička screams at her nephew. "It is a hundred times worse for her!" This is more than Kostelnička can bear, and her anger at Števa for imagining that he can buy himself off with money is portrayed in the orchestral passages that hammer away at Števa's offer of support [132]. This, by the way, is a typical example of Janáček's favored method of composition: deriving his orchestral themes from the verbal inflections of the vocal lines [133].

Kostelnička quickly realizes that angry expostulations will not achieve the desired result, and she now embarks on a long and heartrending attempt to appeal to Števa's better nature. "Števa! Števa! Have pity on Jenúfa! What has the poor creature done to you that you brought her to such dishonor?" [134]. The verbal inflection of "such dishonor":

begins to dominate the musical flow of this section of the drama [135]. Števa is moved to tears. "Auntie," he says, "your words would move a heart of stone!" Nevertheless he refuses to have anything to do with Jenúfa: He is afraid of her; it is not his fault that her face was slashed; he does not love her any more; it is finished, finished; he has become engaged to the mayor's daughter. He becomes downright hysterical, and so does the orchestral accompaniment [136]. Then, quickly taking advantage of the fact that Kostelnička is distracted by Jenúfa, who talks in her sleep, Števa promptly runs away.

The only recourse left to Jenúfa's distraught foster mother is to appeal to Laca, who—as she well knows—feels enormously guilty over the slashing incident and would do anything to win Jenúfa for his wife. But as Kostelnička tells Laca the truth about the baby, Laca becomes momentarily appalled at the thought that he might be saddled with his half brother's son. And in her anguish, Kostelnička blurts out a lie, assuring Laca that the child is dead. Now the die is cast. Sending Laca away on some pretext or other, the unhappy Kostelnička begins to ponder the alternatives open to her. "What if I took the baby and hid it somewhere? No, no! For he would always be a burden, an everlasting shame and dishonor!" It is then that she makes the decision: "So, to the Lord our God I will send the baby!" While the orchestra sings out a mighty hymn-like tune, Kostelnička puts her trust in the Almighty's kindness and justice: "God will surely take him. The baby is too young to have sinned yet!" [137].

At this point her mind begins to wander, and the real reasons behind her action come to the fore. Kostelnička starts having visions of what the villagers would say and do if they knew of her predicament. "How they would taunt me! How they would jeer and taunt Jenúfa! How they would point their fingers at us!"

The orchestra again seizes upon the vocal phrases and keeps repeating them over and over [138]. And now, half insane, and taking advantage of Jenúfa's drugged state, the unhappy foster mother commits the dreadful deed of removing the child from its crib, taking it out of the house, and pushing it under the ice in the frozen river. Here, indeed, we have a very unusual operatic character: a woman whose fear of embarrassment and loss of face induces her to murder a little child. For as she herself says in the third act, after confessing her crime, "I can see now that I did it not so much for Jenúfa's sake as because of my own disgrace!"

While Kostelnička is undoubtedly a most unusual operatic character, the opera *Jenúfa* can boast of an even greater rarity: Laca has the unique distinction of being the only operatic tenor who starts out as a villain and ends up as the hero. One might argue perhaps that his behavior in the first act does not represent his true self. Even so, Laca behaves pretty much like the traditional villain. He goes out of his way to be unpopular and unloved. He accuses Grandmother Burja of discriminating against him; he is nasty to Jenúfa and goes so far as to put worms into her favorite flowerpot to make the blossoms wither. Laca is bitterly envious of his half brother and is aware that Števa is completely unworthy of Jenúfa. Since Laca worships the girl, it kills him to see her head-over-heels in love with this bragging and conceited drunkard. Laca's soul is corroded by jealousy, and his compulsive playing with his knife and constant whittling away at a whip handle are visible symbols of his anger and frustration. In musical terms, this nagging jealousy is represented by repeated notes on the xylophone, which are a prominent feature of the orchestral color of the first act. The peculiar buzzing noise made by the xylophone is in fact the very first sound of the opera [139]. This xylophone passage reappears many times, but it is particularly exposed when an old mill hand sharpens Laca's knife and, at the end of the first act, when Laca becomes quite obnoxious and aggressive.

It is even possible that Laca's slashing of Jenůfa's cheek is not entirely accidental. At the very end of the first act, the old mill hand certainly thinks that Laca has injured Jenůfa on purpose. The slashing is perhaps prompted by a half-conscious urge to prove to Jenůfa that Števa is incapable of real love and that, if she were to become less beautiful, he would lose all interest in her. The ultimate truth about Laca, however, is revealed at the very end of the opera by none other than Jenůfa, who, by rights, should resent him the most. After her whole world collapses around her and Laca still stands by and protects her, Jenůfa finally acknowledges him as the best and finest man she has ever known. As for the slashing of her cheek, "I know now," Jenůfa says in one of the loveliest moments in the final act, "that though you meant to hurt me when you cut my cheek, you sinned only out of love, just as I, too, sinned out of love" [140].

All this surely attests to the truth of the sentiment expressed so well in the enchanting ensemble in the middle of the first act: "Love must bear all its sorrows, and endure them with patience, with patience!" [141].

LUCIA DI LAMMERMOOR

by Gaetano Donizetti

Broadcast December 4, 1982   Cassette illustrations 142–146

EVERYONE KNOWS THAT Donizetti's opera is based on Walter Scott's *The Bride of Lammermoor*, but perhaps not everyone is aware of the differences between the famous novel and the even more famous opera. The heroine of the story, Lucia herself, is left pretty much unchanged in the opera. The members of her operatic family, however, are not at all the same as they are in the novel. The evil genius of Walter Scott's novel is Lucia's mother, Lady Ashton. This haughty and ambitious woman completely dominates all the members of the Ashton clan. She looks down on her weak-willed and vacillating husband; she nurses a deep hatred for all the Ravenswoods and is particularly resentful of Edgar because of his lack of worldly goods, and even more because Edgar comes from a nobler stock than does Lady Ashton's own husband. She has only contempt for her daughter because Lucia is devoid of social ambition and is unwilling to marry the man her mother has chosen for her.

Lady Ashton is described as a truly detestable and diabolical character, perhaps the most detestable mother in all literature. But while such a character is acceptable in a novel, in opera things do not work quite the same way. We do know a few wicked operatic mothers. Mozart's Queen of the Night, who tries to force her daughter to murder Sarastro, is certainly a nasty specimen. Richard Strauss did not object to maternal wickedness in such ladies as Electra's mother, Clytemnestra, or Salome's mother, Herodias. But in Italian operas we do not meet cruel or nasty mothers. The Italian cult of the "loving mamma" does not tolerate stage presentations of cruel mothers. Bellini's Norma, who plans to murder her children, seems to be an exception, but she is not really unfeeling; she loves her boys and cannot force herself to kill them.

Even stepmothers, who have a vested right to be nasty to their stepdaughters, are usually transformed into stepfathers by Italian composers, as, for instance, in Rossini's *Cinderella*. Mothers in Italian operas may be vulnerable and blind, like Gioconda's mother; they may be accused of being witches and burned at the stake, as Azucena's mother is in *Il Trovatore*. They are even permitted to be smarter than their husbands, as Nanetta's mother is in Verdi's *Falstaff*. But they may not be diabolical and detestable. And so, in the opera *Lucia di Lammermoor* Donizetti does away with Lady Ashton. Not only is she dead when the opera starts but we are led to believe that she was a fine person, worth lamenting.

In the very beginning of the opera, the clergyman Raimondo begs Lucia's brother Enrico not to persist in pressing marriage on his sister, because Lucia is a *dolente vergin* ("suffering maiden"), who is still weeping over the recent death of her *cara madre* ("dear mother")! In Donizetti's opera, the head of the family is no longer Lady Ashton. Her role is now entrusted to Lucia's brother Enrico (who also substitutes for Lucia's father and for her other brother, Sholto, who are left out of the opera). Enrico's concerns are legitimate, and we can sympathize with them. He is desperately anxious to escape the political disaster and financial ruin that threaten him because of an impending change in Scotland's government.

In the second act he explains his predicament to his sister. "As soon as Mary ascends the throne the political party to which I belong will be thrown into dust. Only Arturo Bucklaw can rescue me. You *must* marry him, Lucia, and save me from total ruin." When Lucia tells her brother that she is pledged to another man, Enrico becomes vehement and paints a gruesome picture of the consequences of her refusal to marry the rich and influential Arturo. "If you betray me, you prepare the axe for me," he storms. *Ne tuoi sogni mi vedrai.* "You shall see me in your dreams, a raging shadow, the blood-stained axe will always be before your eyes!" That's pretty strong language, and we can imagine the effect such a speech has on an impressionable young girl, especially since she herself is beginning to lose confidence in the fidelity of her lover.

Several months earlier she and Edgardo had sworn eternal faith, *al cielo innante* ("before heaven"). They exchanged rings and promised to write to each other while Edgardo was away on his diplomatic mission in France. The entire final section of the first act is devoted to the joy and anguish of their future love messages. Edgardo has been gone now for many months, and Lucia has not received a single letter. She does not know that Edgardo's messages have been intercepted by her brother. Now she is shown a different document, one that claims that Edgardo is about to marry someone else. Not realizing that the paper is a forgery, Lucia begins to suspect that "that faithless heart has given itself to another woman."

Aware that Lucia's letters to Edgardo have been intercepted by Enrico, the minister Raimondo makes a special effort to acquaint Edgardo with Lucia's predicament. But he also has not received an answer to his message. Not realizing that Edgardo is hurrying posthaste to Scotland, Raimondo urges Lucia to sacrifice herself for her family—for her brother's sake and for the sake of her dead mother. Worn down by all these pressures and by her own doubts, Lucia is finally persuaded to sign the marriage contract between herself and Arturo Bucklaw. It is here that we reach the high point of the drama, the all-important *coup de théâtre*. For no sooner has Lucia signed the marriage papers than a great noise is heard outside, and, to everyone's consternation, Edgardo fights his way past the servants, who are trying to restrain him. Over the stunned silence of the assembled guests, the orchestral winds play a sequence of five chords that seems to be searching for an explanation to the strange intrusion:

Lucia takes a few steps toward Edgardo; she looks at the ring on his finger, gazes at her own ring, and collapses in a dead faint. We have arrived at the famous Sextet [142]!

In an interview with the American writer Arthur Abell, Giacomo Puccini described this sextet as the most famous operatic ensemble number ever written. He also pointed out the peculiarly Italian fondness for treating melancholy and tragic subjects in a major key. "Consider the situation in *Lucia*'s Sextet," Puccini said. "Edgardo and Lucia are in the depths of despair, despair so great that it ends in her insanity and his suicide; and yet what do we find in their vocal parts? Pure honeyed sweetness!"

I am afraid that I must disagree with Maestro Puccini. The Sextet is not about despair, madness, or suicide; it is concerned only with compassion and self-pity. It begins with a duet section for Edgardo and Enrico. Donizetti obviously wanted to make sure that their words would be easily understood and their sentiments clearly revealed. Here are two enemies, vigorous men of action; yet instead of arguing and preparing to fight (as they do in Walter Scott's novel), they indulge in a long introspective meditation. They themselves are surprised at their inability to act; and they ask themselves the same question: "Chi mi frena in tal momento?" "What restrains my anger?" wonders Edgardo. "What restrains my fury?" asks Enrico. They admit that they are overwhelmed with pity for Lucia. I am particularly impressed that Enrico, who was so frantically urging his sister to marry, is now overcome by a strong sense of guilt. "E mio sangue," he sings. "It is my own blood, my own sister! And I am unable to stifle the remorse in my heart" {143}. Walter Scott's Lady Ashton could never have felt and voiced such sentiments.

Eventually Lucia regains her consciousness and laments her inability "either to die or to weep," while all the others observe that "like a wilted rose, she hovers between life and death," and "whoever is not deeply moved by her plight must have a tiger's heart in his breast!" Detractors of nineteenth-century Italian librettos like to make fun of such purple prose, just as some musicians like to point with scorn at such commonplace musical patterns of the *bel canto* style as a guitarlike accompaniment:

or a vocal line sung in parallel thirds and sixths:

But when we consider that *Lucia*'s Sextet—as well as the entire opera—will soon celebrate its 150th birthday without having lost its unfailing, universal appeal, we must concede that the verbal and musical means chosen by Cammarano and Donizetti are more valid than the criticisms leveled against them by their detractors. The occasional verbal and musical clichés of the Sextet do not matter. What matters is that this quiet introspective tableau is an essential architectural component of the final scene of the second act.

From here on, in a carefully structured, step-by-step development, the turmoil and excitement keep intensifying and growing. Having expressed their compassioned concern for Lucia, the men are now ready to use their swords and engage in a fight. But there is a further delay as the minister Raimondo interferes, voicing the general Christian injunction against the use of force: "He who striketh with the sword, shall perish with the sword!" he declaims. The men obey, and sheathe their weapons.

But Enrico still wants to know by what right Edgardo thinks that he can force his way into the domain of the Ashtons. Edgardo claims that his right is based on the oath of fidelity Lucia has sworn to him. When Raimondo shows him the marriage contract signed by Lucia, Edgardo can hardly believe his eyes. He gives his ring back to Lucia and demands that she return the ring he gave her. He wants to know whether she has actually signed the marriage contract. Lucia attempts to explain, but Edgardo does not want to hear any explanations. The only thing he wants to know is whether it is her signature that he sees on the marriage papers. And when the distracted girl admits that it is her writing, Edgardo becomes almost insane in his fury. He curses the day he became her lover {144} and accuses Lucia of being a typical deceitful and dishonest member of the Ashton clan. He draws his sword, attempting to kill Lucia's future husband as well as her brother. He then hits on an even more sadistic ploy for punishing his erstwhile beloved. He throws down his weapon and urges his enemies to kill him, so that the ground on which Lucia is treading will be stained by his blood, and that Lucia, on her way to the altar, would (in the flamboyant words of the Italian text) proceed *calpestando l'esangue mia spoglia* ("trampling over my bloodless remains") {145}.

This wildly exaggerated behavior would be completely out of character for Walter Scott's melancholy and restrained Master of Ravenswood. But his hysterical outbursts provide a wonderful canvas for the fuming

and foaming *crescendos* and *accelerandos* that are a *sine qua non* of every properly constructed finale of an Italian opera. When comparing Walter Scott's
story with Donizetti's opera we must not forget some other important differences. For instance, Edgar's servant, Caleb Balderstone—one of the
most colorful characters of the novel—is not included in the opera. But it
is in the final events of the story that we find the biggest change. The
leading tenor of the opera does not perish by sinking in the quicksands of
his native moor like his Scottish namesake. Rather than having rider and
horse disappear down the stage trap, Donizetti directs the hero of his opera to stab himself among the tombs of his ancestors. Here we will be able
to observe the truth of Puccini's remark concerning the Italian fondness
for setting tragic situations in major keys. A suicide in the jubilant key of
D major will not be found in any French, German, or Russian opera. But
in Donizetti's setting, Edgardo's death scene is heroic rather than sad or
desperate. Edgardo is a man who is on his way to heaven, to join the
woman he loves [146].

THE MAGIC FLUTE

by *Wolfgang Amadeus Mozart*

Broadcast February 7, 1981   Cassette illustrations 147–156

T HE MAGIC FLUTE deals essentially with a power struggle between two mighty adversaries: the Queen of the Night and Sarastro. The conflict is centered on the custody and education of the Queen's daughter, Princess Pamina. The plot seems to follow the time-honored story line describing the battles between the representatives of virtue and the forces of evil. There is, however, a very unusual quirk in this seemingly completely traditional fairytale approach. Those mentioned as being evil during the first half hour of the show, suddenly turn out to be virtuous; and those who seem virtuous in the beginning, are later shown to be wicked.

The reason for this peculiar and unique reversal of roles has never been explained satisfactorily. At one time it was believed that the change was made because the authors of *The Magic Flute*, after completing the first seven sections of the opera, discovered that an operetta entitled *The Magic Zither* was about to be produced ahead of time by a rival theatrical company. Mozart and his librettist, Schikaneder, were presumably afraid to compete with another fairytale that also used magical musical instruments, and they decided to change the story line of their opera. It so happens that this guess has now been completely discredited. For one thing, authors those days were not particularly concerned about the originality and newness of their fairytale operas. Furthermore, it was recently learned that Mozart saw *The Magic Zither* and described it as a hopeless piece of junk without the slightest importance or value.

Other writers have advanced the theory that the story line of *The*

Magic Flute was not changed at all, that right along it had been the intention of the composer and his librettist to present Sarastro as the virtuous and wise ruler and the Queen as the embodiment of evil. The most detailed presentation of this second view was made by the French musicologist Jacques Chailley. In his book *The Magic Flute, a Masonic Work* the author claims that all the events of the opera derive logically from the laws and rituals of the Masonic order, rituals with which both Mozart and Schikaneder were very familiar.

However, even if we grant that Mr. Chailley's evaluation of the Masonic aspect of the opera is correct, from the point of view of the ordinary opera lover—who is not acquainted with and not necessarily interested in Masonic rituals—the opening scenes of *The Magic Flute* unequivocally present the Queen and her three Ladies as helpful and sympathetic characters who have a legitimate grievance against Sarastro. Near the beginning, the Queen is shown as a loving mother, deeply distressed by the abduction of her daughter. In moving words and even more moving music she tells Prince Tamino of having seen her daughter tremble and cry for help: "Noch seh ich ihr zittern mit bangem Erschüttern" [147].

In the spoken dialogue, the abductor of Pamina is described as a powerful and evil magician, capable of changing his appearance into any desired shape. Later, in the Quintet with the Three Ladies, Papageno is certain that Sarastro would pluck out his feathers, roast him on the spit, and then throw his body to the dogs. In contrast to all these reports of Sarastro's evil nature, the actions of the Queen and her three ladies in the opening scenes are benevolent and supportive. The Ladies kill the serpent that threatens Tamino's life, and they give the flute to Tamino and the bells to Papageno. But don't forget that these all-important magical instruments are gifts sent by the Queen. The moral standards of the three Ladies are clearly above reproach. They punish Papageno for lying about killing the snake; and after pardoning him and removing the padlock from his lips, they participate in the first of many pious precepts that make the opera a regular morality play. "Oh," they sing, "if only all liars could have their mouths shut with padlocks; then instead of hatred and false accusations the world would know only love and fraternal unity" [148]. The strains with which these women accompany their praise of music are sincere and moving. "This flute," they tell Tamino, "will protect you and be your safeguard. By means of it you will transform people;

make the sad ones joyful and change ill temper into friendliness" [149].
Finally, the same Ladies summon the three Boys, who are to lead Tamino
and Papageno to Sarastro's castle.

After all these righteous and benevolent actions, what must Tamino
think—and what are we to think—when a while later a venerable Priest
emerging from the Temple of Wisdom tells Tamino that he has been misled; that the Queen, whom Tamino has just described as an "unhappy
woman overcome with grief," is not to be trusted; and that women's
words in general are not to be trusted? Women do little, the Priest says,
except talk, and one should not pay attention to idle chatter. And what
are we to think later, when Sarastro tells Princess Pamina that her mother
is "ein stolzes Weib" ("a proud and arrogant woman"), and then adds a
general statement that by modern standards is most deplorable? "Women,"
Sarastro sings, "must be controlled by men. Without such guidance every
woman tends to stray beyond her assigned sphere." These expressions of
male chauvinism are by no means momentary slips of the tongue. On the
contrary, they are a fundamental point of view expounded by all the
priests of Sarastro's temple. Near the beginning of the second act, two of
these Priests admonish Tamino and Papageno. "Beware of feminine trick-
ery," they sing. "Many a wise man was led astray by women only to find
himself abandoned."

This attitude is immediately adopted by Tamino. In the ensemble
scene that follows, when the three Ladies of the Queen try to arouse the
men against Sarastro, Tamino warns Papageno not to listen to "idle chatter devised by hypocrites and spread by women." Then they all join in,
praising the supposedly calm and unbiased mind of the enlightened male.
"A man," they sing, "thinks before he speaks."

The continuous display of male chauvinism is, of course, much to be
regretted. But Mozart and Schikaneder cannot be blamed entirely for it.
Antifeminist generalizations were an intrinsic part of the cultural climate
of their time. We find them in Mozart's *Così fan tutte*, which is dedicated
to the proposition that no woman can ever be trusted. We find them in
Mozart's *Don Giovanni*, in Masetto's complaints against Zerlina; and even
more so in *The Marriage of Figaro*, where, in his famous last-act aria, "Ap-
rite un po quell'occhi," Figaro assures husbands that all wives are congeni-
tally unfaithful.

In *The Magic Flute* these antifeminist diatribes are directed primarily against power-hungry, politically motivated women, such as the Queen of the Night. Pamina and Papagena, who strive for love, marriage, and motherhood, are treated with respect and are allowed to express themselves in music of great simplicity and charm. For instance, in the first act, Pamina and Papageno sing a celebration of married bliss: "Man and wife, wife and man, reach to heaven hand in hand" {150}; and near the end of the opera, Papageno and Papagena look forward to the joys of parenthood, as the "höchste der Gefühle" ("the most exalted of emotions") {151}.

Even though everything ends happily for Pamina, she has to live through at least two episodes of great suffering. Each time Mozart vouchsafes her music that ranks among the greatest inspirations of all time. I am referring, of course, to the famous aria "Ach, ich fühl's," in which Pamina tells us that if Tamino does not respond to her love, she will seek refuge in death; and to the later scene with the three Boys, when Pamina actually attempts suicide. In the postlude of the Aria, her despair is converted into orchestral sobs that seem to invoke the name of her beloved five times in a row, as if Pamina were silently thinking these words: "Oh Tamino, Tamino, Tamino, Tamino, Tamino, why do you torture me like that?" {152}.

In the Suicide scene, Pamina accuses Tamino of being false to her, and, using the dagger her mother gave her earlier, tries to plunge it into her own heart. This passage seems to me to be the ultimate musical expression of feminine devotion and love {153}. Fortunately the three Boys intervene in time and stop Pamina's desperate attempt to end her life. Then all four of them join in uttering still another of the many sentimental vignettes of our fairytale: "Zwei Herzen die von Liebe brennen, kann Menschenohnmacht niemals trennen" ("Two hearts that love has bound together, no human frailty can sever"):

zwei Herz - en, die   von Lie - be bren-nen

But now, let us consider once more the question I raised earlier, namely, whether there was in fact an unexpected change in the basic plot of the opera and if so, the reason for it. My own guess is that, at first, Mozart and Schikaneder were planning to follow the traditional outline of fairytales, and have Tamino and Papageno defeat Sarastro with the help of the magic flute and the magic bells. They were then to restore Pamina to her mother and celebrate a double wedding between Tamino and Pamina, and Papageno and Papagena. This plot sequence was followed through the first episode in Sarastro's castle, where the cruel and lecherous Moor, Monostatos, is quite logically seen as a member of Sarastro's wicked gang. It seems to me that the text—and what is far more important—the music of the initial sections of the score unquestionably support this point of view. If Mozart had thought of the Queen and her three Ladies as hypocritical and nasty characters, he certainly would have written a very different kind of music for them.

But when the authors arrived at the eighth section of the first act, the scene with the three temples, they realized the advantages of a more serious approach, involving solemn choral scenes and impressive fire and water tests, patterned on Masonic rituals. Once they had decided to transform Sarastro into a wise and virtuous leader, it became necessary to invent some special wickedness for the Queen of the Night. What was more natural than to have her invade her enemy's castle and try to induce her daughter to murder Sarastro! To justify Tamino's change of heart, the authors had to stress the basic unreliability of female accusations, most particularly the fact that the Queen's testimony could not be trusted. Considering the sudden flip-flop between the virtuous ones and the villains, between the goodies and the baddies, a general antifeminist tone becomes unavoidable.

The Magic Flute is filled with moral utterances—copybook sentiments regarding liars, marriage, the need for discretion, and so on. The most impressive of these pronouncements takes place in the fifteenth episode of the second act, when the two armor-clad guardians of the temple read the inscription written on the gates that protect the entrance to the ordeals of fire and water. First, the orchestral strings portray the suffering and turmoil of humanity: the laborious striving upward [154] and the lamentations of those who fall behind [155]. Then, along with the inces-

sant web of orchestral climbing and lamenting, we hear the voices of the
armored men, supported by wind instruments, as they sing the Chorale
melody:

Der,   welch-er   wan-dert   die - se   Stras-se   voll Be - schwer - den

The words of the Chorale use Masonic symbols, but they obviously have a
general validity. "He who travels this road filled with hardships will be
purified by fire, water, earth, and air. Those who succeed in overcoming
the fear of death, will be able to join the initiates of the temple and will be
able to devote themselves fully to the mysteries of the goddess Isis." This
entire vocal and orchestral ebb and flow has a solemnity and a moral fervor
that are without parallel, not only in Mozart's operas but perhaps in the
entire operatic literature {156}.

There is still another moral lesson in *The Magic Flute*, one that I discovered more or less accidentally. Many years ago, I produced a series of
one-hour operas for children. I chose the segments to be sung and acted,
and, between the musical sections of each standard work, I would explain
the situations and fill out the plot. *The Magic Flute* was perhaps the most
successful of these shows. Everybody loved Papageno and Papagena; the
costumes for the Queen, the Prince, and the Princess were colorful and
exciting; and the musical numbers I selected were short and did not tire
the youngsters. Since I was fortunate enough to have a very good-looking
Queen of the Night with a fine voice, I always included her second-act
aria, in which she forces a dagger into her daughter's hand and commands
Pamina to murder Sarastro. If Pamina should refuse to do so, the Queen
threatens to disown and curse her.

At the end of this aria, after the Queen had left the stage and the
applause had subsided, Pamina would stand there with the dagger in her
hand, saying: "No! I refuse to do it. I cannot commit murder!" At this
point I would step forward and address the audience. "You see children," I
would say, "from this you learn that there are certain things you must not
do, even if your mummy tells you to do them!" You can imagine the effect
of my words. The whole place would freeze in shocked disbelief. The children were afraid to look at their parents; mothers did not dare to look at
their children. I would let them stew in horrified silence for a few moments and then take them off the hook by saying: "Of course, you chil-

dren have nothing to worry about. Your mummies would never tell you to do anything of the sort."

What struck me, however, was how vividly Pamina's predicament illustrated the profound truth we had to digest during the Nürnberg trials following the Second World War; namely, that one's own personal sense of right and wrong can never be totally abdicated, and that acts of inhumanity cannot be justified by the excuse of having to obey other people, no matter what their position of authority might be.

MANON LESCAUT

By Giacomo Puccini

Broadcast March 21, 1981   Cassette illustrations 157–173

No ONE HAS DESCRIBED Manon's essential character more justly and eloquently than the French novelist Guy de Maupassant. In his admirable disquisition on women, this connoisseur of the female soul has this to say:

> Let us look at Manon as if we had actually met her and loved her. We perceive the clear cunning look which seems always smiling and promising; we know the lively false mouth, the small teeth within the tempting lips; the fine penciled brows, the vivacious and coaxing movement of the head, the charming motion of the figure, and the fresh fragrance of the youthful body. No woman has ever been so womanly—or ever contained the quintessence of her sex, as this celebrated girl so sweet and so perfidious. As soon as Des Grieux met her he became by simple contagion, by the mere contact with the depraved nature of Manon, a cheat and a scoundrel!

Maupassant was not speaking of the opera *Manon Lescaut* or of any other musical version of the story. He was referring to the novel by Antoine François Prévost, from which Puccini's opera is derived. The main theme of this famous eighteenth-century romance is the gradual destruction of a fine, upright young man by a tantalizingly lovely but thoroughly unscrupulous woman. To give this theme maximum impressiveness, the author endowed the victim with very strong initial defenses. Young Des Grieux comes from a good family. While still a boy, he was enrolled in the order of the Knights of Malta and took the required vows of celibacy. He has been attending a religious seminary and has reached the age of seventeen without—as he himself puts it—having given much thought to the difference between the sexes. As soon as young Des Grieux catches sight of Manon he is struck as if by lightning and with surprising rapidity turns, as Maupassant put it, into a cheat and a scoundrel—and worse! He steals, gives up a promising ecclesiastic career, and excels as a professional cardsharp; he becomes a gigolo, poses as Manon's younger brother, and lives on the money and jewelry Manon extracts from her various lovers. He sinks ever more deeply into the cloaca of moral corruption, crowning his criminal career by murdering a prison guard while escaping from jail. Unable to shake off his amorous obsession, he pretends to be Manon's husband and in this guise succeeds in following Manon on her deportation trip to Louisiana.

As one compares this sequence of shady events with the story of Puccini's opera, one is amazed at the difference in the depiction of Des Grieux's character. His gambling *is* mentioned by Manon's brother soon after the curtain rises on the second act, and Des Grieux himself alludes to it rather fleetingly in the course of his stormy love duet with Manon. But that is all. We neither see nor hear anything of Des Grieux's activities as a gigolo, impersonator, jailbird, or murderer. Puccini documents his amorous obsession in dozens of magnificent vocal phrases, but otherwise Des Grieux is surprisingly passive. In the third act he makes one desperate attempt at forcibly freeing Manon from the guards who are about to take her away to the extradition ship, but he gives up immediately.

All in all, there is surprisingly little skulduggery or physical violence in the opera. That is quite unlike the Puccini we know from his late works, where, beginning with *Tosca*, we are regaled with escapes, pursuits, cheating at cards, impersonation of a dead man, falsification of wills, tortures, stabbings, executions, and stranglings; not to mention five suicides (four of which take place in full view of the audience) and other fanciful acts of aggression, including the beheading of several princely heads in *Turandot*. I suspect that Puccini was interested in Des Grieux only to the extent that Des Grieux is infatuated with the lovely Manon. It is only in the third act, when Des Grieux is faced with the seemingly unavoidable prospect of losing his beloved, that Puccini really gets excited about him and lets him give vent to a magnificent and wildly passionate musical and emotional outburst wherein the desperate lover implores the captain of the ship to let him go to America with Manon and the rest of the crew [157].

Throughout the opera we feel that the composer, no less than the tenor, is fascinated with and deeply in love with the fickle heroine of his opera. Except for the opening of the drama—the relatively short section before the arrival of the interurban coach transporting the heroine—everything that happens relates to her and only to her. We are shown the most diverse and contrasting sides of her colorful, beguiling, and wicked nature. In the first act we witness her shy conversation with an attractive stranger [158]. Later, we are perhaps a bit surprised at the ease with which she permits herself to be abducted by the young man she met only a few minutes earlier, and at how readily the timid little-girl tune presented earlier turns into the triumphant victory shout of the liberated woman [159].

Throughout the duration of the second act, Manon never leaves the stage. We are repeatedly shown the two basic aspects of her personality: her fascination with the pleasures of love and her love for the fascinating pleasures that she can obtain with money. It is most instructive to observe how these contrasting sides of Manon's character—the amorous side and the money-loving side—are reflected in her music. Her love of luxury is, stylistically speaking, pure eighteenth-century rococo; while the strains that accompany her yearning for Des Grieux's caresses are borrowed from the techniques we associate with the second half of the nineteenth century, more particularly with Wagnerian romanticism. For instance, when Manon is at her toilette, making up her face [160], or being entertained by a group of madrigal singers [161], or learning how to dance a courtly Minuet [162], the music is of the "galant" style, the musical badinage that was so popular with the wealthy music lovers in the period preceding the French revolution.

But when, in between these lighthearted activities, Manon begins to recollect her delights in the arms of her young lover, the standard classical harmonies quickly dissolve into sequences based on various inversions of chords of the seventh [163]. Later, when Manon is forced to exert all her seductive charms in order to mollify her justly angry lover, there are numerous episodes featuring chords of the ninth progressing in sequences that cannot help but make us think of the exotic and metaphysical pas-

sions of Tristan and Isolde [164]. Speaking of unusual harmonic progressions, there is a spot near the end of the opera where Puccini tries his luck
with a string of descending augmented triads, a musical idea that was
considered extremely daring at the time the opera was composed. The passage occurs when Manon assures Des Grieux that the flame of her love is
about to be extinguished [165].

Puccini may have been in love with Manon, but he was not about to
gloss over her defects. In the second act he lets us observe some of her
brazen and foolish behavior, actions that lead directly to her undoing.
When her elderly protector, Geronte, catches her making love to Des
Grieux and accuses her of ingratitude, especially after he has showered so
much love on her, she taunts him sadistically. "How can *you* have the
nerve to speak of love?" she asks, holding a mirror in front of Geronte's
face. "Look at yourself, and then look at us, before speaking of love"
[166]. And then she laughs uproariously, rejoicing that she had gotten rid
of the elderly gentleman and his so-called amours [167]. Later, she is so
anxious to collect as many jewels as possible, that she forfeits her chance to
escape from the soldiers summoned by Geronte [168]. In the third act, we
see a much more attractive and gentle side of her character, when Manon
tries to console Des Grieux and advises him to forget her and return to his
father [169]. (This, by the way, is the only time that Puccini mentions
Des Grieux's father, a character who plays a very important role in the
original story and in Massenet's setting of the same subject.)

The most moving episode in Manon's checkered career takes place in
the last act. While there are many musical echoes of amorous effusions
that occur earlier, the gem of this final act is Manon's tragic monologue.
Manon laments her fate after being left alone on the arid plain while Des
Grieux tries to find shelter and water for his exhausted companion. In the
opening measures she intones the sentence by which this solo is identified:
"Sola, perduta, abbandonata" [170]. Immediately after this opening
phrase, Puccini starts experimenting with a very unusual instrumental
idea, letting the oboe phrase in the orchestra be echoed by an offstage
flute. Coupled with the obstinately repetitious harmonic sequences in the
strings and the mournful vocal line, this duet produces a most desolate
effect [171]. The final section of the monologue features a very gripping
passage, which is quite different from anything that has issued from
Manon's lips so far [172]. Manon sings here of people who wanted to tear

her away from her lover; she also mentions that Des Grieux has shed someone's blood, and that it was her own ill-fated beauty that brought her to
this final disaster.

All this is quite puzzling and requires a bit of explanation, especially
since many opera lovers wonder what Des Grieux and Manon are doing in
that desert in the first place. According to the stage direction in the score,
the setting represents a vast plain outside New Orleans. But it was certainly understood that Manon and the eleven other girls who were put
aboard the deportation ship in the third act were not sent to Louisiana to
wander on the outskirts of New Orleans. Clearly, these ladies of questionable virtue—some of whom bear such sonorous operatic names as Rosetta,
Madelon, Regina, Violetta, and Giorgetta—are expected to help populate
a remote outpost of the French colonial empire.

In Prévost's novel, upon their arrival in New Orleans, Manon and
her lover pretend that they are man and wife. They are cordially accepted
as such and welcomed by the leaders of the community. All goes well until Des Grieux has qualms and decides that he and Manon should get married in fact as well as in name. As preparations for the church wedding are
being made, it becomes obvious that Des Grieux is not Manon's husband,
and the governor of Louisiana announces that he has other plans for
Manon. Since she has been sent to Louisiana to help the colonials, she has
to marry a fine local fellow, none other than the governor's own nephew,
Synnelet, who is greatly impressed by Manon's beauty. A quarrel ensues,
and Des Grieux and Synnelet fight a duel. Synnelet is severely wounded;
in fact, Des Grieux is under the impression that he has killed him. The
lovers decide to flee New Orleans, and that is why, when the curtain rises
on the fourth act, we find them in that desolate, waterless plain.

I am occasionally asked where Puccini found an arid plain on the outskirts of New Orleans, when to the best recollection of the inhabitants,
there has never been anything of the sort down there. I guess we'll have to
ascribe it to poetic license. Anyway, as long as we let Shakespeare invent a
sea coast in Bohemia and allow Bizet to erect mountains on the outskirts
of Seville, I am willing to close one eye and accept a desert outside New
Orleans, provided that I may keep both ears open to listen to Manon's
monologue in the last act [173].

DIE MEISTERSINGER VON NÜRNBERG

by Richard Wagner

Broadcast December 28, 1968   No cassette illustrations

DURING THE CLOSING ensemble of the first act of *Die Meistersinger von Nürnberg*, the assembled Masters pronounce judgment on Walther von Stolzing and his trial song. "Versungen und verthan" ("failed and rejected") are the last words they sing, summing up their contention that Walther's song does not live up to the rules which, in their opinion, must govern a work of art. How many times in his own stormy career was Wagner himself judged in a similar manner by the critics and the public? The composer had to spend the greater part of his days fighting those who accused him of writing wrong, incorrect, faulty music. "Versungen und verthan" was indeed a chorus that in real life rang many times in the composer's bewildered ears.

There is no doubt that the plot of *Die Meistersinger* is to a large extent a reflection of Wagner's own experiences, of his own struggles as a creative artist. And maybe it is just because the opera mirrors so closely Wagner's own sufferings, disappointments, and hard-won victories that it is such an exciting, deeply human document. It is well to keep in mind that Wagner's basic problem here is one that confronts every young artist and that recurs in every generation—the conflict between new artistic ideas and old ones.

The artistic ideas of the past are, of course, represented in the opera by the Mastersingers, the older generation of settled and successful citizens who believe in established academic rules and who insist on respect for the traditions and procedures inherited from the past. These artistic ideas are also represented by a music critic, Sixtus Beckmesser, who is undoubtedly the most celebrated music critic in history. When Richard Wagner created the character of Beckmesser, he definitely had one particular live model in mind: the Viennese music critic Eduard Hanslick, famous today as the man who made life miserable for Richard Wagner. I am sure that every young artist feels complete sympathy for Walther von Stolzing, whose first recital is, so to speak, watched over by that terrifying music critic with his chalk and blackboard, who keeps score on every violation of the rules and whose judgment could make or break the poor neophyte.

Well, if in Beckmesser Wagner painted the picture—or rather the caricature—of his critical opponent, he undoubtedly painted a picture of himself in Walther von Stolzing, that impetuous youthful artist whose genius breaks the rules of the past and who eventually wins out over the petty criticisms of Beckmesser and the reactionary older Mastersingers. Wagner went out of his way to present Beckmesser as a repulsive person who is envious of Walther's appearance and talent and who tries very hard to look and act like Walther, without succeeding in the least. This becomes quite apparent in the themes Wagner allotted to these two candidates for Eva's hand. He gave Walther a noble-sounding theme:

Beckmesser's appears to be a pitiful attempt to imitate Walther's music and make Beckmesser look and behave like a noble cavalier:

In order that we not miss the point that the critic, Beckmesser, is eager to look and behave like the artist he is judging, Wagner constantly presents these two themes in close proximity. This is true not only in the first act, when both men are onstage at the same time, but also in the first scene of the third act, when Beckmesser is alone in Sachs's shoemaker shop. As he enters the shop, he is still smarting from the beating he received the preceding evening:

and when he thinks of Walther he explodes in a jealous rage:

Identifying Beckmesser with Hanslick and Walther von Stolzing with Richard Wagner does not by any means uncover all of the hidden meaning in the opera. By 1867, when Wagner wrote *Die Meistersinger*, he was already well past the early storms of his youth. He was well in his fifties, certainly no longer the young hero of his *Tannhäuser* and *Lohengrin* days. There is another person in *Die Meistersinger*, an older man of a more settled character, who has an even greater kinship with Wagner. I mean, of course, Hans Sachs. He represents the more mature Wagner, the man who not only values flaming, soaring imagination but also realizes the importance of established rules and the service these rules have rendered to the continued progress of the arts.

Die Meistersinger, perhaps more than any other musical work I know, represents this reconciliation of the old and the new, of traditional procedures with revolutionary, radically novel ideas. At first glance, this opera seems to be just another old-fashioned operatic comedy. In fact, Wagner planned it as a comic opera, easy to perform and gay enough to attract popular fancy. And it cannot be denied that the work is full of stock characters and situations typical of the old improvised *commedia dell'arte* and of *opera buffa*. As in all Italian comic operas, there is a pair of young romantic lovers—Eva and Walther; and a pair of comic servants who are confidential advisors of the lovers and help with a little intrigue—David and Magdalene. There is the menace—the ridiculous, pompous, unwelcome suitor, Beckmesser, who is no different from Doctor Bartolo in Rossini's *The Barber of Seville* or from Doctor Caius in Verdi's *Falstaff*. And there is the girl's father—Pogner, who, like Ford in *Falstaff*, is a father who makes it easier for the unwelcome suitor, in our case, for Beckmesser.

There are many other ingredients that can be found in every *opera buffa*: quarrels, serenades, and mistaken identities. There is also another stock character who is important in all these comedies—the friend and helper of the lovers. Like Figaro in *The Barber* or Dr. Malatesta in *Don Pasquale*, he manipulates the plot so that it comes out in favor of the young people: it is Hans Sachs. We can be forgiven, of course, for not thinking of Hans Sachs as a stock character of *opera buffa*, for here is the exact point where Wagner's radically new concept of comedy becomes apparent. It is Hans Sachs who changes *Die Meistersinger* from light, popular entertainment into a work of art, into a human drama for all time. For Wagner took this stock type, the helper of the young lovers, and infused him with his own problems, making him not only part of the emotional involvement but the real hero of the play.

Through this hero, Wagner develops one of his favorite themes, that of masculine renunciation. It is a theme that was very dear to Wagner, and he developed it in several operas. For instance, Wolfram renounces his love for Elisabeth in favor of his friend Tannhäuser, and do not forget the noble figure of King Marke. In the third act of *Die Meistersinger* Sachs recalls the story and the music of *Tristan und Isolde*:

and declares to Eva that he would not welcome the fate of old King Marke:

But, most important of all, it is Hans Sachs who teaches Walther to respect the old traditional rules of poetry and of the craft of musical composition.

These established rules are extremely rigid. No wonder that a young genius like Walther von Stolzing cannot see why it should be so important to press a song into two verses of equal length, of parallel construction, and of similar melodic content—two *Stollen*, as they are called in the rule books of the Mastersingers—and why these two *Stollen* have to be followed by an *Abgesang*—an after-song, a chorus, so to speak, double in length and different in material. A young genius can never see the need for rigid rules, but Hans Sachs, the mature artist, knows that lawlessness and chaos cannot be tolerated. His great mission in the opera is to reconcile the wildness of Walther's imagination with the orderliness of the traditional forms.

This strict application of codified rules is historically correct, of course. Wagner carefully studied the rule books printed in the sixteenth century by the Nürnberg Mastersingers. The special poetic structure which is preached and enforced so vigorously in the opera—two short verses of equal length and a chorus twice as long happens to be one of the oldest forms known to poetry. The ancient Greeks used it and the not-so-ancient Americans still use it. Many a Broadway hit song uses the same form—two short verses and a chorus.

In the first scene of the third act, there is an important conversation between Sachs and Walther. The older man explains to our young poet the reason and purpose of this construction. As Sachs so charmingly puts it, the two verses are like a married couple, alike and yet somewhat different. And the *Abgesang*, the chorus, is like their children, who are of a different generation, yet show a family resemblance to the parents. This idea is immediately reflected in the first stanza of the Prize Song, which Walther improvises on the spot. The first two verses begin alike:

but continue in a slightly different fashion. The much longer *Abgesang* is quite different, yet shows a certain resemblance to the verses:

The idea of two short verses followed by a much longer chorus is old and elementary, but Wagner had the almost incredible audacity to apply this construction to an entire five-hour music drama. It has been pointed out that the first two acts of *Die Meistersinger* correspond to two *Stollen*, or verses, and that the last, much longer act, constitutes the *Abgesang*, the after-song, or chorus. One does not have to be a learned musicologist to notice the resemblance between the culminating events of the first two acts. Everything that happens in the first act leads to the examination scene, as we may call it, to Walther's song, by means of which the young knight hopes to come closer to winning Eva's hand. This song, interrupted by the strokes of Beckmesser, the Marker, leads in turn to the choral ensemble, to the chaotic squabble involving Walther, the Masters, and the apprentices. The second act has exactly the same kind of culmination: Beckmesser's Serenade, by means of which Eva's other suitor hopes to come closer to winning her hand, is interrupted by Sachs's hammering on his shoes. It also leads to a chaotic "fight scene" involving the entire ensemble of singers.

In addition to these obvious occurrences, practically every detail of the first act has a corresponding parallel event in the second act. Being aware of this parallel construction, by the way, is not just an exercise in ingenuity and a clever analysis of details. Realizing that the second act is something of a mirror picture of the first act, really helps us to follow the complicated events of the second act. I say "mirror picture" because the situations presented seriously in one act are usually treated humorously or ironically in the other. For instance, the first act begins with a solemn church chorus, which is combined with a flirtatious pantomimic exchange between Walther and Eva. The second act also opens with a chorus—the gay chorus of the apprentices—and it is also interrupted by, and combined with, chatter between the other two lovers, the apprentice David and Eva's nurse, Magdalene. In other words, what was a serious and romantic scene in the first act, becomes a gay and somewhat farcical episode in the second act.

Later in the first act, David tries to enlighten Walther about the thousand and one rules that have to be learned and digested by an aspiring singer-poet-composer before he can hope to be admitted into the select company of the Masters. In the corresponding section of the second act, Hans Sachs makes the startling observation that even though the examination song Walther presented in the first act did not fit any of the rules ("keine Regel wollte da passen"), it seemed faultless ("war doch kein Fehler drin"). Where David, like so many apprentices in the arts, is impressed only by accumulated erudition based on perspiration, Hans Sachs has an innate feeling for intuition and inspiration.

To return to the first act, Walther questions David about his chances for qualifying as an applicant in the competition for Eva's hand. Walther then declares, "So bleibt mir einzig der Meisterlohn" ("then I must aim straightaway for the Master's degree"). The idea that someone expects to get to the very top without taking all the intermediate steps seems so presumptuous to David and the other apprentices, that they make fun of Walther, wishing him "Good Luck" on trying to become, so to speak, an "instant Mastersinger." In the corresponding episode in the second act, Eva questions Sachs about Walther's success in his examination, and Sachs makes the ironic observation that "Wer als Meister geboren, der hat unter Meistern den schlimsten Stand" ("one who is born a Master hasn't much of a chance with the established, professional masters"). What was meant sarcastically in the first act, turns into bitter wisdom in the second act.

These parallels and analogies between the two acts continue to the very end. Just before the first act curtain Hans Sachs is alone on stage listening to the echoes of Walther's song and of the quarreling chorus. Well, at the very end of the second act, it is the Night Watchman who remains all alone, listening to the echoes of Beckmesser's song and of the fight chorus. One wonders whether Wagner planned all this. Did he deliberately set out to make this whole opera into one gigantic mastersong, complete with two *Stollen* and an *Abgesang*? I, for one, don't really believe that Wagner used this construction intentionally. But what do we know about the secret workings of a genius? Maybe Wagner was so filled with the ideas he put into this great work, that mysteriously and without his planning it, the opera took on the form prescribed in the old rule books of the Mastersingers.

Be that as it may, *Die Meistersinger von Nürnberg* is so magnificent a creation that we cannot ignore any ideas that might help us to penetrate its vastness. There are always new discoveries, new joys, new revelations in this immense work, from whose pages Wagner, the greatest Mastersinger of them all, speaks to us not only with the flaming genius of Walther von Stolzing but also with the mature wisdom of Hans Sachs.

PARSIFAL

by Richard Wagner

Broadcast April 9, 1960   Cassette illustrations 174–181

IF THE WORLD had obeyed Richard Wagner's instructions, this performance of *Parsifal* at the Metropolitan Opera House in New York and this broadcast would not be taking place. So solemn is the story of *Parsifal*, so devotional is much of its music, that Richard Wagner, during his lifetime, did not permit any performances of the work outside of the festival auditorium he had built for the exclusive presentation of his works in the little Bavarian town of Bayreuth. All his other works Wagner relinquished to the rest of the world, but *Parsifal*, he felt, required a special atmosphere, an attitude of concentration and reverence on the part of the audience that could not be achieved in the hustle and bustle of everyday life. According to Wagner, only the special setting of Bayreuth would meet these needs. In a letter to his protector, King Ludwig of Bavaria, Wagner wrote: "*Parsifal* should never be produced merely for the entertainment of an audience."

Literally speaking, Richard Wagner's wish has not been obeyed: *Parsifal is* being performed all over the world. But in a broader sense, his intentions are still being fulfilled. Wherever *Parsifal* is performed, be it in the quiet surroundings of Bayreuth or in busy New York, it is always presented and received the way the composer named it so fittingly: a festival dedication play for the stage.

What is it that gives *Parsifal* this special quality and makes its presentation traditional during Christianity's most sacred week? To be sure, there is a very close connection between Christian symbols and beliefs and many elements of the story and music of *Parsifal*. Near the end of the first act, solemn strains accompany the unveiling of the Grail—the cup from which Jesus drank at the last supper and into which Joseph of Arimathea received the blood of the Saviour upon the cross. The theme of the Grail—heard just before the curtain comes down—contains a direct quotation from a celebrated piece of liturgical music, the Dresden Amen:

During the last scene of the first act, the unfortunate Amfortas presides over the ceremony in the temple of the Knights of the Grail. He suffers in his body from a never-healing wound and in his soul by a remorse that makes him unfit to fulfill the exalted obligations of his office, namely, the unveiling of the Grail. This ceremony contains many elements of the Communion service—the Eucharist. The transformation of the bread and wine is accompanied by one of the basic musical themes of *Parsifal*, known as the Motive of the Eucharist [174], and throughout the opera, the following theme symbolizes Faith:

Another relic kept by the Knights of the Grail is the Holy Spear, which once wounded Christ on the Cross and which is presented musically by its own unforgettable phrase [175]. The loss of the Holy Spear by Amfortas and its recovery by Parsifal is the main theme of the story of this work.

These are some—but by no means all—of the roots which hold the story of *Parsifal* firmly in Christian soil. However, the work contains additional ideas that are related to Christian thinking but not directly derived from it. Wagner has also incorporated in this work some of the great ethical concepts that were developed early in the nineteenth century by the German philosopher Arthur Schopenhauer, whose writings made a deep and lasting impression on Wagner. Schopenhauer's most important ethical principle is the idea of compassion as the basic element of human morality.

The German word for compassion, *Mitleid* (*Mit* = with, *Leid* = suf-

fering), means co-suffering—suffering with another being. To Schopenhauer, the sharing of pain and suffering with others and the determination
to alleviate such pain and such suffering are responsible for every truly
ethical, unselfish deed. He contrasts this principle of compassion with
malice, an evil state of mind which delights in the suffering of others.

In *Parsifal*, Wagner applied Schopenhauer's philosophical theories to
the practical life of the stage and created characters which clearly represent
Schopenhauer's opposing ethical principles of compassion and malice.
Malice is represented by Klingsor, who once tried to qualify as a Knight of
the Holy Grail. But his heart was not pure, and he was refused admit-
tance. Since that time, Klingsor has been filled with rage and bent on
vengeance. He has obtained the power of magic, created a luscious garden
in the wilderness, and filled it with beautiful women, who lure the
Knights of the Holy Grail from virtue.

As the opposite pole to the evil Klingsor, Wagner conceived the pure
figure of young Parsifal. The rugged music that portrays the dangerous
power of Klingsor [176] stands in great contrast to the lofty, noble music
that represents Parsifal [177]. Parsifal is the ideal fulfillment of Schopenhauer's conception of a being, guided by *Mitleid*, by compassion. It is not
only that Parsifal wishes to alleviate the anguish of others. As the play
progresses, he actually reaches a point where he suffers the pain of his
fellowmen in a mystic process of complete identification. Such a person
must be pure in heart and experience the full impact of compassion with
every fellow human being. But he must feel it by instinct, not through a
process of reasoning or intellectual discovery.

Before he even enters the stage, Parsifal is already described as such a
person. Gurnemanz speaks of the one who will come to heal Amfortas's
wound and who will restore the waning powers of the Grail. In his Prophecy, help will come only from him who is, in Gurnemanz's words, "ein
reiner Tor" ("a pure fool") [178]. However, the German word *Tor* does
not really mean a foolish person—it rather means a simple person, someone who is innocent and unspoiled.

Parsifal's first action in the play is the killing—the senseless killing—of a swan. As Gurnemanz reproaches him, Parsifal, in the words of
the score, listens with growing emotion. As the old man asks him
whether he realizes the magnitude of his sin, Parsifal—and this is important—answers: "I did not *know* it was wrong." He did not know; he is,

indeed, guileless. But already compassion begins to make him knowing. As Gurnemanz describes the suffering of the swan, we hear the theme of compassion:

Overcome by remorse, Parsifal breaks his bow and hurls his arrow to the ground. He will not kill wantonly again.

This new feeling of compassion takes rapid possession of Parsifal's pure heart. It reaches a much fuller expression in the second scene of the first act, the temple scene, in which Parsifal witnesses the suffering of Amfortas—his bodily pain and his mental anguish. As Parsifal hears the tormented man's cry of agony, he suddenly clutches his own heart and, in accordance with Wagner's stage directions, remains in a petrified, motionless position as if he, too, were feeling the pain of the wound. A more advanced state of compassion has now been reached: the process of identification with the suffering of another person.

But even this is not enough to give Parsifal the powers that the real, ultimate feeling of compassion will bestow on him. Parsifal's purity and his ethical determination have to be put to the test. In the second act, when Parsifal enters Klingsor's magic garden, he follows in the steps of Amfortas, who once came here to battle Klingsor, only to be seduced by Kundry and defeated in his holy mission. Parsifal is now put in exactly the same situation that brought about the downfall of Amfortas. While Amfortas was clutched in the embrace of Kundry, the Holy Spear was snatched from his hand by Klingsor. And at the very moment that Kundry's lips touched his, Amfortas suffered the never-healing wound.

This time, it is Parsifal who sinks down in Kundry's embrace. Her arms around him, she touches his lips in a long kiss, which is meant to make him unfit for his exalted mission. But Parsifal starts up, suddenly, with a gesture of intense suffering and terror. His looks alter fearfully, he presses his hand tightly against his heart as if in the throes of an agonizing pain, exactly as he heard Amfortas's cry of agony in the first act. And then Parsifal cries out: "Amfortas!"

Here is complete identification with another human being's pain. It is true *Mitleid*, co-suffering. Parsifal's compassion has proven stronger than his lustful desires. It is from this very act of compassion that Parsifal, from now on, derives his power. In resisting the lures of Kundry, in setting the image of the suffering Amfortas between himself and temptation, Parsifal has won the strength to vanquish the evil might of Klingsor.

In the third act, Parsifal returns to Montsalvat, to the accompaniment of the celebrated Good Friday music [179]. He has gained wisdom through compassion and has become worthy to assume the high office of leading the Knights of the Grail. The earlier, exuberant and innocent Parsifal has mellowed into a more serious, more mature, more knowing person [180]. Parsifal returns with the Holy Spear, and in the Grail Scene of the third act, he heals Amfortas and restores the power of the Grail. But it is not through the spear alone that the miracle of healing is accomplished. It is power bestowed through compassion on the pure and simple soul that conquers evil and washes away the wounds that evil has inflicted. As Parsifal takes over his duties as the spiritual leader of the Knights, he once more reiterates the source of his strength. The music of the Prophecy is heard again, but what was once a mere promise of salvation is now a glorious reality [181].

It is suffering and the full measure of compassion—not knowledge, wisdom, strength, or any qualities of the mind—that are the source of goodness. Here the philosophy of Schopenhauer, as projected by Richard Wagner in this great work, is close to the basic teachings of many of the great religious leaders of mankind. In the final analysis, the whole story of *Parsifal* is contained in a few simple words that were spoken almost 2,000 years ago on a mountainside near the Lake of Tiberias: "Blessed are the pure in spirit for theirs is the Kingdom of Heaven."

PELLÉAS ET MÉLISANDE

by Claude Debussy

Broadcast March 4, 1978   Cassette illustrations 182–193

EVERY YOUNG COMPOSER of opera yearns to find the operatic text of his dreams, the text which will give full expression to his particular talents. Claude Achille Debussy was no exception. As the 26-year-old Debussy confided to his friend and teacher, Ernest Guiraud,

> Some day I will find my poet! And that poet will be content to speak in a whisper, content merely to hint at beauty, to suggest with words what my music will fulfill. And that poet will not cramp his play into long, artificial acts, but will write short, fluid episodes. And his characters will not argue endlessly, but will submit to destiny. . . .

Four years later, Debussy's prophesy was fulfilled, and in Maurice Maeterlinck he found his poet. *Pelléas et Mélisande* proved to be in every detail the operatic text of which Debussy had dreamed.

Maeterlinck's play elaborates a subtle variation of the ancient fairy tale in which a princess, magically transformed into a graceful animal—a swan or a gazelle—is waiting for a hunter, a prince charming who, by wounding her slightly, returns her to a human shape. The unusual aspect of Maeterlinck's play is that, by an accident of fate, the princess, Mélisande, is disenchanted not by her predestined prince charming, Pelléas, but by his half brother, the widower Golaud. This leads to a tragic complication in which the three characters involved stumble in the dark like blind people. Unable to understand what has occurred, they—in Debussy's words—"submit to destiny."

Maeterlinck's play is replete with symbols of darkness and light, of blindness and intuitive awareness. At the end of the third act, little Yniold begs his father to lead him into the lighted room. But Golaud says that he prefers to remain in the shadows until the full truth is revealed. Among the symbolic concepts that are given special musical images are the pitch-black entrance into the grotto of the sixth scene of the first act [182], and the sudden rays of moonlight that illuminate the scene and reveal three beggars sleeping in the grotto [183]. Debussy's orchestra constantly enchants us with the contrasts between gloomy darkness and brilliant radiance. In the eighth scene of the first act, it sets the mood when Pelléas and Golaud inspect the dank and oppressive caverns [184]. A little later, when they emerge into the open landscape, where the fresh breeze is coming from the sea, the blowing of the wind is faithfully portrayed in the music [185]; and when Pelléas remarks that, in the distance, at the seashore, he can see children about to take a swim and that the noonday bells are beginning to chime, the laughter of children and the ringing of the bells are represented by the orchestra with superb clarity [186]. With the fountain in the park that had the miraculous quality of curing blindness, Debussy had a perfect opportunity to show off his unique virtuosity for the musical portrayals of everything connected with water, whether in the form of splashing spray, falling drops, or streaming rivulets [187].

Maeterlinck's play is full of events and references that help establish and maintain this otherworldly atmosphere of dimly perceived truth: the single rose blooming in the shadows, mists rising from the sea, ships passing in the distance, the wedding ring accidentally or not so accidentally dropping into the well. All these images contribute to the mysterious quality of the chiaroscuro—the play of shadow and light—that gives the opera its special quality. No wonder that Debussy described Maeterlinck's sensitive language as "so moving, so suggestive, that it created music of its own accord." But Debussy's music for *Pelléas,* which one critic compared to "a bowl of green olives," was not a taste which Debussy's contemporaries found easy to acquire.

What right, they demanded, did this strange fruit of Debussy's absurd musical and dramatic theories have to be called "opera"? Was it not true that in the second scene of the first act, as Geneviève reads aloud Golaud's letter to Pelléas, Debussy set 18 consecutive words—28 syllables—on the same single monotonous note?

le troi-siè-me jour qui sui-vra cet-te let-tre, al-lume u-ne lampe au som-met de la

tour qui re-gar-de la mer.

Where were the impassioned vocal melodies like those of Gounod and Bizet, or the stirring arias that could serve as display pieces for the great voices of generations to come? No, it seemed all too apparent to his contemporaries that Debussy's way of writing for the voice was far too radical, too new, ever to become popular. But the truth was that Debussy's theories of vocal expression were not new at all; on the contrary, these theories were so old that they had almost been forgotten.

Yes, Debussy would have found a far more congenial welcome some 300 years earlier in Florence, at the home of Count Giovanni Bardi, at whose dinner table it is said that opera was born. Count Bardi gathered around him a little group of the leading poets and musicians of the town. They called themselves the *Camerata* ("Cabinet"), and they held regular meetings in the hope of restoring the grandeur of Greek tragedy and of determining the esthetic principles that governed it. But like Christopher Columbus, they did not discover precisely what they were looking for. And, like Columbus, they quite inadvertently stumbled upon a new world, the world of opera.

But time brings many changes. Just as it is doubtful that Columbus would now recognize the land on which he first set foot, so there can be no doubt that the distinguished members of Count Bardi's *Camerata* would be enormously astonished to hear the bright vocal melodies of Verdi, Puccini, or Bizet. For to the *Camerata*, vocal melody was not an end in itself but the obedient servant of the words to which it was attached. They quoted Plato, the great Greek philosopher, as saying, "The musician should use his melodies to garnish the poet's verses, just as a good cook adds a pungent sauce to make a dish more savory." So these musical cooks in Florence conscientiously copied in their melodies the characteristic rise and fall of speech. The end result was a vocal line which sounded very much as though the words were being recited aloud.

This recitation style, or *recitative*, as it came to be known, was very much what Debussy set out to achieve in his *Pelléas et Mélisande*. Of course he was not satisfied with a vocal line which merely imitated the sound of words. More important, he insisted that his vocal line also portray the feeling which lay beneath the word, the undercurrent of emotion which brought it to the lips. As long as the feelings of a character were controlled, they could be expressed in a vocal line which itself was controlled. But when the emotions of the character expand, the melodic line must expand as well. As Debussy himself put it, "Melody begins where words are no longer adequate."

In *Pelléas* we have ample opportunity to observe instances of these expanded melodic outbursts. They occur most frequently, fittingly enough, in the love scenes, as in the seventh scene of the first act, when Pelléas, standing underneath the tower, caresses Mélisande's hair, which has just cascaded down from the window where she is standing [188]. There is another wonderful vocal phrase in the last scene of the second act. Mélisande has just confessed to Pelléas that she loves him, and Pelléas describes in this moving phrase the effect her voice has on him: "It caresses my ears like gentle music, and it falls like fresh water on my lips" [189]. Certainly such passages cannot be accused of monotony in vocal treatment.

Now although Debussy's vocal and melodic ideas dated back to the beginning of opera, his harmonic theories were something else again. Many of the harmonies Debussy used not only *sounded* strange and new, they *were* new, shockingly new! And by their consistent use, Debussy struck a mighty blow at the core of musical theory which generations of composers—Mozart, Beethoven, and Verdi, included—had considered implicit in the very nature of music. For many centuries Western music had been built on a system of scales, the same familiar scales which long-suffering school children still practice so diligently:

Sometimes whole melodies have been built around consecutive notes of these scales. Take, for example, the beloved Christmas carol *The First Noel*:

or Gilda's famous aria from Verdi's *Rigoletto*, "Caro Nome":

Ca-ro   no - me che il mio   cor   fe-sti pri - mo pal - pi - tar

These scales are constructed according to strict rules that were actually handed down from earliest antiquity. These rules were always considered so sacred that their infringement—believe it or not—resulted in severe punishment. For example, according to the rule book, a proper scale is constructed in two parts; each part is called a *tetrachord* and consists of four notes:

The authorized distances between the notes of the tetrachord were the whole tone and the half tone. But—and here is the rub—there could be only *two* consecutive whole tones within each tetrachord. The third consecutive whole tone was felt to produce such an evil sound that it was known as *diabolus in musica* ("the devil in music"), and its use was actually forbidden by church law!

Debussy was not afraid of this particular "devil," and it can be found on practically every page of *Pelléas*. In fact, the very scale Debussy uses most often in the opera is made up entirely of whole tones:

Debussy, with his whole-tone scale, not only introduced the "devil," the third consecutive whole tone, but used the fourth and fifth consecutive whole tones as well! The theorists had not even contemplated the existence of these "devils" and, therefore, had not had the foresight to prohibit them!

This whole-tone scale accounts for much of the characteristic color of *Pelléas*. Long sections are written entirely in this idiom. For example, in the introduction to the eighth scene of the first act, the Vault Scene, weird patterns of unrelieved whole-tone music depict the dark, gloomy dampness of underground caverns [190]. Another passage occurs at the very beginning of the opera, when Golaud wonders if he will ever find his way out of the forest where the pursuit of the wounded animal had led him {191}.

The harmonies that result from combining various notes of the whole-tone scale do not sound or behave like traditional harmonies. The most typical harmony this scale produces is the augmented triad, as opposed to the familiar major triad:

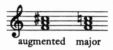
augmented   major

Now, by using the whole-tone scale and the augmented triad, you can make almost any tune sound as if it came from *Pelléas*. Even "My Country 'tis of Thee" can be clothed in this strange disguise:

and I wonder what Verdi would think of his "Caro Nome" camouflaged by the whole-tone scale:

While the whole-tone scale and its harmonies are responsible for much of the distinctive color of the music of *Pelléas*, they do not by any means explain it all. Debussy did not hesitate to use traditional scales and traditional harmonies, but he used them in ways that traditional theorists would hardly have approved! For they maintained that certain chords have in their very nature a tension, an incomplete unresolved feeling which gives them an undeniable impulse to lead forward, to resolve into other chords:

tension   resolved

whose nature creates a feeling of finality and repose.

There is a legend that Mozart (a notoriously late sleeper) was roused out of bed one morning by a whimsical caller who went to the piano and played a succession of three chords:

But then he stopped! Mozart's ears could not stand the suspense. He leapt out of bed, rushed to the piano, and completed the sequence!

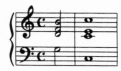

It is very likely that Debussy, in a similar situation, would just have turned over and gone back to sleep. Even as a young student, Debussy had highly individual views regarding chords. The story goes that he was once called into the office of the registrar of the Paris Conservatory and interrogated because of his strange views. "I hear," said the registrar, "that you claim that dissonant chords need not be resolved. May I ask what rules you follow?" "Indeed," replied Debussy, "I follow the rules of my pleasure." It was often Debussy's pleasure to take a simple chord, based on the first, third, and fifth notes of the conventional scale:

and add to it another note—a sixth perhaps, or a ninth. The most shocking thing (from the conventional point of view) was that Debussy delighted in leaving these strange formations unresolved, hanging in the air, and even used them to end movements of compositions! It was with just such a chord that he brought to a close the third scene of the first act {192}. Debussy loved these ninth chords so much that he often wrote whole strings of them. One such sequence occurs in the first act, when Pelléas and Mélisande are watching the mist rise from the sea {193}. These ninths appear so often in *Pelléas* that a caustic French critic nicknamed the opera "Le Pays des Neuvièmes" ("The Country of the Ninths").

Debussy was not alarmed by criticism. As he himself put it, "When a man of genius breaks with tradition, the world is certain to be incensed. The only thing that is left for the poor man of genius to do is to die young, and this is the only manifestation of his genius which his contemporaries applaud." Although Debussy was quite firm in his ideas concerning the way *he* wished to compose music, he did not ask that others follow his example. "When I listen to a new work," he said, "I try to forget all other music I have heard before, for fear that my ears, accustomed to old familiar sounds, be deafened to the beauty of the new."

Let us approach *Pelléas et Mélisande* in that spirit—with fresh ears and fresh eyes—so that we may capture the unique beauty and magic which this poetic and imaginative play with music contains, for, in the words of Claude Achille Debussy, "Music, of all the arts, is the most susceptible to magic!"

PETER GRIMES

by Benjamin Britten

This opera, with its justly famous sea interludes, deals with a tug of war between an eccentric human being and his environment. Peter Grimes is eager to get rich by "fishing the sea dry"! This is the only way, he feels, to become accepted by the inhabitants of the small Suffolk village and to be able to marry the local school-teacher, Ellen Orford. The sea is equally eager to destroy Grimes, but wishes to do it on its own terms, in calm weather. During a recent storm, Grimes lost an ap-prentice under suspicious circumstances. He is warned not to take another teenaged helper, but with Ellen Orford's assistance he manages to find another boy. When Ellen discovers that Grimes has been maltreating the child, she quarrels with him. Grimes takes the boy to his hut on a cliff top, but the popular feeling against him rises to such a pitch that the entire village sets out after them. When Grimes and his helper try to escape by another route, the boy falls to his death down the cliff which was eroded during the earlier storm. Three days later Grimes turns up in the village at dawn. He is at his wits' end, and a retired sea captain, Balstrode, advises him to sail his boat out to sea and sink it. Grimes does so, as the village comes to life for another calm and ordinary day.

Broadcast February 11, 1967   Cassette illustrations 194–208

WHY IS IT THAT some operas remain in the repertoire and are in de-mand year-in and year-out, while others disappear after a season or two and join the thousands that are known only as titles in dictionaries or as dusty tomes on library shelves? It seems to me that one of the most impor-tant features of a truly successful opera is an abundance of a certain type of music, music that keeps haunting us, that sticks in our minds, and that eventually becomes part of our permanent, musical heritage. As I discovered many years ago, *Peter Grimes* is unusually rich in such memorable and memorizable tunes.

My own association with this opera goes back to the summer of 1946. Serge Koussevitzky commissioned the work and saw to it that it was performed in Tanglewood in a very carefully prepared and effectively mounted American première. We started rehearsing the opera early in July and by the end of the month, every student of the Berkshire Music Center—whether he was actively involved in the production or not—was heard singing, humming, or whistling quite a number of its tunes, such as "Old Joe has gone fishing" or "We live and let live, and look—we keep our hands to ourselves!" [194].

There were several other tunes that "took possession" of us. Most of them are related to the idea of "gossiping," which is such an important dramatic motive of this opera. Two that appear in the second act are "What is it? What is it? What do you suppose? Grimes is at his exercise!" [195], and the stirring marching tune sung in unison by the chorus with the accompaniment of the drum: "Now is gossip put on trial" [196].

A third tune of this type occurs in the Prologue:

It opens the opera and plays a very important part in the scene of the inquest. Near the end of the second act, however, it acquires a particularly memorable slant because of the words sung by Swallow, the Mayor of the Borough. After all the men arrive at Grimes's hut and find no evidence of any mischief, Swallow says, "Here we come pell-mell, expecting to find out—we know not what. But all we find is a neat and empty hut. Gentlemen, take this to your wives: *less interference in our private lives!*"

Gen-tle-men, take this to your wives: __ less in-ter-fer-ence in our pri - vate lives

The purely instrumental portions of *Peter Grimes* also feature a number of thoroughly haunting passages that stick to our musical minds, par-

ticularly the orchestral interludes that describe the sea, which is so inex-
tricably tied up with Grimes and with the other inhabitants of the
Borough. The sea is depicted in its many aspects: the calm sea with crying
seagulls, wavelets rushing to the beach, and the deep surge of the surf
beating at the shore:

and the stormy sea, with the wind whipping the waters and the moaning
that sounds as if some wounded monster of the deep is lamenting in endless, abysmal pain [197].

The musical passages have a direct and immediate appeal, but Britten is not satisfied with the mere invention of impressive musical phrases
and catchy tunes. Having been "caught" by this music we discover, sooner
or later, that Britten, like every other serious composer, manages to give
his ideas additional musical and dramatic significance. "Old Joe," for instance, is soon joined by two other tunes:

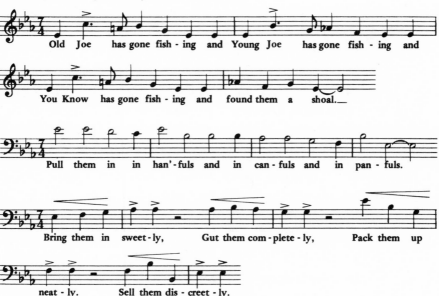

and the counterpoint and interplay of these three melodies, weaving in and out through all the voices from the bass to the treble, give this sea chanty its shapeliness and musical variety. Furthermore, this chorus is made to serve an important dramatic purpose. When Grimes joins the singing, he almost manages to upset the entire musical apple cart. His very personal treatment of the tune is characteristic of his unwillingness or inability to conform to ordinary rules of civil behavior. Instead of becoming part of the singing ensemble, he disturbs and antagonizes his fellow singers, gives the melody a different rhythm, and sings it in keys not related to what the others are doing.

At first the refrain of "Grimes is at his exercise" seems to be just an expressive and trenchant phrase to describe the Borough's negative reaction to Grimes. But it is the same phrase that Grimes hurls at the world after his quarrel with Ellen: "And God have mercy upon me!"

And God have mer - cy up-on me!

Later it becomes the foundation of the so-called Passacaglia interlude, which connects the two scenes of the second act. In this interlude, eleven orchestral variations are superimposed on the identical theme played in the bass [198].

This combination of purely sensual appeal and more profound, almost intellectual significance, reminds me of Mozart's saying that in his operas he always tried to please the ordinary, untutored listener, but that at the same time he was also aiming to provide more subtle satisfactions for the ears of the connoisseurs. I suspect that this desire is also at the root of Britten's operatic attitudes. He is perfectly willing to follow traditional procedures, but he invariably manages to give them a very special and unexpected twist.

Britten's highly original touch in presenting familiar dramatic and musical devices is apparent in the opening scene of the second act, where a church service conducted offstage is preceded by the ringing of bells and then combined with important dramatic actions played on the square outside the church. The gay ringing of bells and the glitter of sunshine create a festive and brightly shining Sunday morning mood [199]. The melody which Ellen Orford sings here is shaped in an enormous musical arc that soars over an octave and a half like the blue and brilliant arch of heaven stretching from one end of the sun-lit sky to the other: "Glitter of waves and glitter of sunlight" [200].

When the service begins, Ellen and Grimes's young apprentice remain outside. She tries to draw the boy into friendly conversation, but when she discovers that his shirt is torn and that he has an ugly bruise on his neck, she begins to suspect that Grimes has been too rough with him and has perhaps been maltreating the lad. She attempts to console the youngster with the thought that today, at least, he can have a holiday and rest up from his daily chores.

At this point, Grimes enters, looking for his apprentice. He has sighted an enormous shoal of fish and feels that this is his chance of hauling in the catch that will make him wealthy. When Ellen reminds him that he promised not to have the boy work on Sundays, Grimes insists, saying: "This is whatever day I say it is! Come boy! He works for me, leave him alone, he is mine!" In spite of Ellen's efforts to calm him, Grimes refuses to give in. The argument turns into a violent quarrel at the end of which Grimes strikes Ellen and walks off chasing the boy ahead of him. This scene holds the central spot in the opera, and its gradual progress from the radiant holiday mood to the ugly climax of the quarrel is handled in a truly masterful fashion, both dramatically and musically.

What I find particularly fascinating here is that every aspect of the stage action has its exact counterpart in the words and music of the church service being sung offstage. Ellen's early attempts to draw the boy into conversation coincide with the *fermatas* that end each of the chanting phrases of the opening anthem. This is the same device that Wagner employs in the opening scene of *Die Meistersinger*, where the flirtation between Eva and Walther is similarly made to coincide with the *fermatas* of the chorale sung by the congregation [201]. Britten begins this scene with the same procedure [202] but then expands this particular idea so that it covers the entire church service from the opening anthem to the final Amen. At the point at which Ellen discovers the torn shirt and the bruise on the boy's neck, we have reached the antiphonal responses, during which the rector and the chorus alternate singing: "Most merciful Father, we have erred and strayed from Thy ways like lost sheep. And we have done these things which we ought not to have done."

When Ellen urges the boy to enjoy his day of rest, saying: "Let this be a holiday full of peace and quietness," the congregation sings: "The Lord's name be praised":

Grimes's entrance coincides with the agitated section of the singing of the Psalms. When Peter says: "I've seen a shoal. I need help; I can see shoals to which the rest are blind," from the church comes this excited chanting: "O, ye winds of God, bless ye the Lord; O, ye lightnings and clouds, bless ye the Lord, praise him and magnify him forever" [203]. And even more to the point, the chorus chants later: "O, ye seas and the Floods, bless ye the Lord; O, ye Whales and all that move in the Waters, Praise Him and magnify Him forever!" At the end of this scene, after Peter has struck Ellen, the congregation sings Amen, and Grimes echoes it by saying: "So be it! And God have mercy upon me!"

Grimes's rough treatment of his apprentice and particularly that shocking moment when he loses his temper and strikes the girl he loves are incidents that highlight the main dramatic problem of the opera, namely, how to make Grimes into a man who deserves the sympathy of the audience. In George Crabbe's poem "The Borough," from which many incidents of this opera are taken, Grimes is a thoroughly despicable person without a spark of decency or kindness. Britten's Grimes is a completely different sort of human being. Underneath his violent and explosive exterior, he is sensitive and capable of affection and tenderness.

There are at least two places in the opera where he reveals his inner, more gentle self, where he dreams of a "harbor that shelters peace," and sings of his craving for domestic happiness. At the end of the first scene, Grimes has a conversation with Balstrode, after which a furious orchestral storm breaks loose. Remaining alone on the stage, Grimes puts his faith in Ellen and his love for her: "With her there'll be no quarrels, with her the mood will stay. Her breast is harbor too, where night is turned to day!" [204]. Even more touching and tender is Grimes's soliloquy near the end of the second act, when, ashamed of his roughness with the boy and Ellen, he dreams of future happiness: "I've seen in stars the life that we might share; fruit in the garden, children by the shore, a whitened doorstep, and a woman's care!" [205].

There is no denying, of course, that Grimes is a violent character, different from the others, an outsider. Single-handedly he fights two formidable adversaries: the citizens of the Borough and the sea that surrounds it. His tragedy is that he yearns to belong to these people, to be one of them, but he does not know how to make himself liked by them. He pretends to despise his fellow men and particularly their women. He wants to marry Ellen Orford, but he resents the idea that she might accept him out of pity! And so, he wants to "fish the sea dry," to become the "rich merchant," but for that he needs money. He spells it out in his conversation with Balstrode, near the end of the first scene of the opera: "These Borough gossips listen to money, only to money!"

These Bor-ough gos-sips lis-ten to mon-ey, on-ly to mon-ey.

And so money becomes an obsession. To get money, Grimes must conquer the sea, but his relationship with the sea is also a tragic one. All his misfortunes are directly traceable to the power of the sea.

The death of Grimes's first apprentice, which takes place some time before the opera opens, is a direct act of malevolence on the part of the sea. We are told that Grimes was lured by the huge catch of fish, and no sooner did he sail the boat around the coast with the intention of putting into London, than the wind turned against him and blew him off his course. For three days the sea kept him, until the drinking water was all gone and the apprentice died. The storm, which starts at the end of the first scene and continues through the second, causes a landslide and creates the precipice which is responsible for the death of Grimes's second apprentice. Thus, the sea gradually drives Grimes insane, until he finally commits suicide by sinking his boat in calm weather. One feels that although the ocean could destroy Grimes at any time, it chooses to win him in its own way!

And what of the citizens of the Borough who turn against Grimes? They are basically decent, ordinary people, but in Grimes they sense an alien being, incomprehensible and dangerous. After Grimes's visionary monologue in the Inn Scene, all they find to say is: "He's mad or drunk! His song alone would sour the beer!" But it is in the Lynching Chorus of the last act that they voice their deeper objections to him: "He who holds himself apart, lets his pride rise. And cruelty becomes his enterprise! Him who despises us, we'll destroy! Our curse shall fall on his evil day, we shall tame his arrogance!" What makes the Lynching Chorus particularly telling is that the musical themes that underlie these chants of hatred are the very same tunes to which, just a short while earlier, these people dance their gay dances. The good-natured tunes of the Gallop [206] and of the Country Dance [207] transform themselves with surprising and frightening ease into sounds of mass hysteria sung by a blood-thirsty mob bent on destruction and killing [208].

Peter Grimes is an unusual story told in a new and compelling musical language. Benjamin Britten accomplishes in this work the fundamental aim of great art: to teach us something new about the human heart and express it through original and significant musical beauty.

RIGOLETTO

by Giuseppe Verdi

Broadcast January 19, 1980   No cassette illustrations

W E KNOW FROM Verdi's letters to his librettists that he was constantly on the lookout for stories that exhibited unusual situations filled with colorful incidents and unbridled passions. I think that it is fair to say that no other subject chosen by Verdi fitted this description as well as Victor Hugo's *Le Roi s'amuse*. The "Roi," the "king" who "amused himself" in Victor Hugo's drama, was Francis I of France. But when the play was converted into an opera, the Venetian censor forced the composer and his librettist to transform the French king into an Italian duke and to move the action from Paris to Mantua. It is in this form that Verdi's *Rigoletto* has been known ever since.

Victor Hugo's historical and political allusions were lost in the process, but his radical dramatic ideas remained intact. There is no doubt that 150 years ago, when Hugo started his career as a playwright, his theatrical notions were indeed revolutionary. In the preface to his first major drama, *Cromwell*, Hugo announced that his plays would no longer parade protagonists who were either all-virtuous or all-villainous. Instead, he would introduce a different kind of contrast and choose characters who might be physical and moral monsters but who would, at the same time, be magnanimous, kind, and gentle. Hugo described such complex characters as grotesque creatures.

There is no doubt that the protagonist of the opera *Rigoletto* is a worthy representative of this grotesque tribe. In his capacity as court jester, Rigoletto is ugly, hunchbacked, mean, and sadistic. He hates the courtiers, and it delights him to encourage the Duke to seduce their daughters and wives. He even occasionally suggests to his master that the Duke might consider beheading a husband or a father who proves to be a bit too recalcitrant. But Rigoletto has another, much different side. In his private life he is a loving father, neurotically anxious to protect his adored daughter, Gilda, from all possible harm. These grotesque contrasts are brilliantly illustrated in Verdi's music. In the opening scene, we hear the orchestral equivalents of Rigoletto's jumps and gyrations:

and his grisly laughter as he taunts Monterone, the aggrieved father of a seduced daughter:

Compare these with the heart-rending melodies Rigoletto sings in the second scene, when he tells Gilda that her dead mother was the only human being who had ever been kind to him:

El - la sen - tia, quel-l'an - ge-lo, pie - tà____ del - le__ mie pe - ne...

Earlier, in the second scene, when Rigoletto describes himself as deformed and wicked, the orchestra seconds his clownish gestures with equally graphic musical grimaces:

How different is Rigoletto's behavior and his music in the next act, when he comforts his daughter and attempts to dry her tears: "Weep, child, let your tears flow on my heart":

Pian - gi,   pian - gi, fan - ciul - la, fan-ciul - la, pian - gi.

While the jester is undoubtedly the most bizarre figure in the opera, he is by no means the only complicated one. Even the skirt-chasing Duke, who would be the last person to form a sincere attachment to any of his female victims, exhibits occasional touches of remorse and decent feeling. One occurs at the opening of the second act, in the recitative preceding his aria. The Duke reminisces about his meeting with Gilda: "When she gazed at me with that innocent expression, I felt a spark of tenderness and constancy suddenly surging in my breast. I believe that I was almost impelled toward virtue!" We know, of course, that the Duke's virtuous resolutions are only a fleeting aberration, but while they last the sincerity of Verdi's music certainly makes them surprisingly convincing:

co - lei che pri - ma po - tè in que - sto co - re de - star la

fiam - ma di co - stan - ti af - fet - ti?

Much more grotesque is the "murder-for-hire" brother-and-sister gang of Sparafucile and Maddalena. The brother is a regular "hit" man, who, for the price of twenty gold coins, can be hired by anyone to dispatch an enemy or a rival. Even so, when his sister suggests that instead of killing their current guest, it would be so much simpler to murder the fellow who commissioned the deed, Sparafucile becomes indignant: "Kill the hunchback? What are you saying! Am I a thief, perhaps, or a bandit? The fellow has hired me, his work shall be done." And in his vocal phrase one feels the pride of the honest artisan:

Mi pa - ga que - st'uo - mo,   fe - de - le m'a - vrà.

Yet a bit later, to oblige his sister, who keeps badgering him, Sparafucile abandons his "honest artisan" pretensions and agrees to cheat his employer and kill a substitute if a visitor should present himself in time. And what about Maddalena, who undoubtedly has been acting for quite some time as her brother's assistant and willing accomplice? Why does she suddenly become soft-hearted and protective? One has the feeling that, in the past, her brother's victims were mostly so old or unattractive that she did not care what happened to them.

This evening, however, the man to be dispatched is young and handsome, and moreover he has offered to marry Maddelena. This matrimonial offer is heard in the midst of the conversation in the Quartet in the last act. Maddalena tells her guest that his amorous declarations are only meant to tease her. "No, no," the Duke says, "ti vo sposar" ("I want you for my wife!"). It is rather surprising that Maddalena should take this obviously ironic remark seriously. And yet, she does! "Ne voglio la parola," she keeps repeating. ("Give me your word of honor; say you really mean it; say it again!") But maybe it is not as surprising as all that. Gilda, who eavesdrops on this conversation through a crack in the wall, knows perfectly well that the ridiculous offer is made in jest, by a married nobleman in search of extramarital adventures. But Maddalena is not at all aware of it. As far as she is concerned, the fellow who is proposing to her is a handsome cavalry officer with a saber in his belt and spurs on his boots, just the sort of guy she was always hoping to marry someday. It also points up that this street-dancing Maddalena, who was trained by her brother to lure men into his tavern and to lead them on with amorous play, is in reality pathetically unsophisticated.

It is curious that opera audiences always think of sopranos as being pure maidens and of contraltos as Delila-like or Carmen-like temptresses. When watching the final scene of *Rigoletto*, opera lovers are likely to imagine that Gilda is the innocent virgin, while Sparafucile's sister is little better than a harlot. I am, on the contrary, fairly certain that Maddalena—who is watched day and night by her big brute of a brother—has never been touched by a man, while Gilda not only loves the Duke and believes that she is loved by him but, what is more to the point, has been living in sin with him for the last month. A girl in love Gilda certainly is, but an innocent virgin? No, sir!

The presence of these strangely complicated, grotesque characters is only one aspect of *Rigoletto* that makes it different from all other Verdi operas. It has several other very unusual distinctions. To begin with, the leading baritone role is unquestionably the most demanding and difficult in the entire Verdi repertoire. Throughout the opera Rigoletto brims over with the most violent passions: sinister ill-will, superstitious fear, abject self-pity, helpless rage, and murderous glee. Rigoletto hates the Duke, loves his daughter to distraction, plans a murder, rejoices in vengeance, and weeps in disaster. And while singing his heart out the baritone has to portray a hunchbacked cripple, and that means that throughout the entire opera he must maintain a crooked posture that puts an additional severe strain on his physical equilibrium and his vocal mechanism. Another, less demanding but still curious, feature is the absence of a women's chorus. *Rigoletto* is the only Verdi opera in which all the choral singing is done by the men. The male choristers not only sing and act the roles of the courtiers in the first two acts but also participate in the storm music of the third act by humming offstage to imitate the moaning of the wind:

Perhaps the most peculiarly challenging task in the opera is imposed on the lighting designer, who, at one point, must create the impression that the stage is enveloped in pitch-black darkness and yet somehow make the movements of the actors visible to the audience. The scene occurs near the end of the first act, and the whole situation is bizarre, to say the least. The courtiers, wearing masks and bearing lanterns assemble outside the wall of Gilda's garden. Just as they get ready to climb the ladder they brought with them, they hear Rigoletto singing offstage. Quickly the lanterns are extinguished, and the resulting darkness is so profound that, as Rigoletto enters, he actually bumps into Borsa, one of the courtiers. Eventually, Marullo, another courtier, succeeds in convincing Rigoletto that the group of masqueraders is involved in a plot to abduct the Countess Ceprano, whose palace is located across the street from Gilda's garden. Much relieved, Rigoletto is only too willing to put on a mask, join the others in their prank, and assist them by holding the ladder. As Marullo helps Rigoletto to don the mask, he also manages to tie a scarf over the jester's head, a scarf thick enough to make Rigoletto blind and deaf. The lanterns are then re-lit and the courtiers are able to proceed with their original plan of abducting Gilda.

It is not easy to make this sequence of events believable. Imagine how efficient the blindfold has to be for Rigoletto not to notice the lanterns being lighted or hear the courtiers whispering their "Zitti-zitti" chorus inches away from him. But think how complete the darkness has to be *before* the mask is put on Rigoletto, if he is not to become aware that he has been blindfolded! Short blackouts are not unusual in the theater, but this sequence of events is the only one I can think of where, for the sake of dramatic credibility, a nearly total blackout must be maintained for a full minute and a half.

This scene is not the only one in *Rigoletto* in which darkness and partial invisibility play an important dramatic role. In the last act, at the very moment when Gilda crosses the threshhold of the tavern to be stabbed by Sparafucile, the stage direction in the score instructs Maddalena to run downstage and close the front archway, through which the audience has been seeing the inside of the tavern. At this point, according to the score, "Tutto resta sepolto nel silenzio e nel buio" ("Everything is buried in silence and darkness"). When the opera was first produced, over a century ago, the light was cut off to protect the spectators from the indecorous ordeal of seeing a young girl stabbed in the chest. Today's theatergoers are less squeamish, and, as a rule, it is only after the clearly visible stabbing that Maddalena extinguishes the lantern so that the rest of the action inside the tavern can become invisible.

Whether we actually see it or not, we know, of course, that while the storm is raging outside, the stabbed victim is stuffed into a sack which Maddalena was mending earlier in the scene. I often wonder what must pass through Maddalena's mind when she discovers—as undoubtedly she must in the process of handling the body—that the substitute victim is not a beggar boy (as Maddalena has been led to believe) but a young girl dressed in a riding habit with boots and spurs. I know that audiences seldom concern themselves with the reactions of characters whom they can neither see nor hear, but Maddalena's shock of discovery, even though invisible, is still one more grisly event in the grotesque plot of the opera.

During this invisible action, while the substitute body is being readied for delivery, the tempest, which has been raging for quite a while, reaches its climax. All the theatrical storm paraphernalia available to the producer are put into operation: wind-and-thunder machines, augmented by drumbeats offstage, as well as projections of sheets of rain and of various types of lightnings. Not only is this storm the longest and probably the most violent in the entire operatic repertoire but also it serves several special dramatic and musical purposes. Its imminent approach early in the

scene gives the Duke a good excuse to ask to be housed in the tavern. The
storm also enables Verdi to introduce the offstage humming, which, when
the tempest finally begins to subside, creates an especially telling effect in
conjunction with the orchestral woodwinds. But what makes this storm
truly unusual is that it is preceded by a type of weather in which rain is
not actually falling but tiny gusts of wind are followed by soft rumbles of
thunder and by distant lightnings that illuminate the landscape for a
couple of seconds. To interpret these phenomena in musical terms, Verdi
creates a subtle sequence of orchestral events: first, an almost inaudible
tremolo in the violins, representing the rustling of the wind; next, the
zigzagging lightnings, which are always initiated by the flute and completed by the piccolo;

followed by distant thunder, executed by the lower strings assisted by a
backstage drum; and, finally, the moaning of the wind, depicted by the
invisible male chorus.

　　This combination of musical events, which is first heard soon after the
Quartet section, is repeated at various times and in different keys. All this
not only prepares us for the coming major storm but also sets up some
sensational *coup de théâtre* effects that take place after the body in the sack is
delivered to Rigoletto. At that point, the jester experiences three crushing
emotional shocks, cunningly envisioned by Victor Hugo and eloquently
elaborated by Verdi. At first Rigoletto has no inkling that he has been
cheated. He is tempted to inspect the contents of the sack but sees no
reason to do so since—to his mind—the spurs that stick out of the sack
obviously belong to the Duke. The presence of these spurs, by the way, is
the dramatic *raison d'être* behind the Duke's cavalry uniform and Gilda's
riding habit. Then, just as Rigoletto starts to drag the sack toward the
river, he hears the Duke singing his regrets that Maddalena has not come
to let him make love to her:

The realization that the Duke is alive unleashes the first emotional thun-
derbolt. Wondering why a substitution had been made, Rigoletto cuts

open the sack, but in the darkness (and here again we must imagine how dark it has to be) he is unable to distinguish any features. Now comes the so-carefully prepared flash of lightning. To his horror, Rigoletto sees his daughter's face, and we have the second emotional explosion:

In the darkness that follows the all-too-short flash of lightning, Rigoletto imagines that he has had a hallucination. Certainly, Gilda has to be on horseback at this moment, on her way to Verona. It is the next flash of lightning that finally convinces Rigoletto that the body in the sack is actually that of his own daughter.

The seemingly lifeless Gilda revives and, in the final pages of the score, sings some of the loveliest music of the entire opera. People who do not care for opera enjoy making fun of the fact that severely wounded characters who are on the brink of death are capable of giving forth very demanding vocal efforts. To answer this, I like to point out that fatally wounded people do not necessarily die instantly, but often survive for quite a long time. Furthermore, opera, by definition, is a theatrical event, where, instead of speaking (or even thinking), actors sing with orchestral accompaniment. In this form of art—with which all of us are so much in love—people are expected to sing just as long as they can whisper or think. And isn't it wonderful that, instead of whispering or thinking, Gilda can regale us with such gorgeous vocal melodies as:

Las - sù in   cie - lo, vi-ci-na al-la ma-dre   in e -   ter - no per voi pre-ghe-rò

RISE AND FALL OF THE CITY OF MAHAGONNY

by Kurt Weill

Broadcast December 22, 1979   Cassette illustrations 209–215

THE PRESENTATION OF the opera *Rise and Fall of the City of Mahagonny* is in many respects unlike any other Met broadcast in the last forty years. Even its name is not what you might imagine. It is not ma-hog'-a-ny, and it has nothing to do with the reddish brown wood we know by that name. It is an invented word pronounced Ma-ha-gun'-ny. It is the name of a city; and since I also had some difficulty getting used to this pronunciation, I trained myself by saying: "Ma-ha-gun'-ny is a place of milk and honey to which the main character comes with lots of munney and at the end is sentenced to the electric chair because of a lack of munney."

The librettist of the opera—the famous German poet and dramatist Bertolt Brecht—was infatuated with names that have a similar rhythmic pattern, and his text is replete with such names as Alabama, Pensacola, San Francisco, and Oklahoma. The presence of these American place names is not accidental. In Berlin, in the late 1920s, when *Mahagonny* was written, German artists were fascinated with the United States. They knew about Prohibition, speakeasies, and the electric chair. To quote Kurt Weill, the composer of the opera: "They had also read Jack London and they knew everything about Chicago gangsters. So, of course, when they did a fantasy, it was about America."

Germany was just emerging from a galloping inflation that completely wiped out its entire economic system. I was in Berlin then, newly arrived from Russia, and my mother happened to have a few American dollars. For a single dollar we could get several million German marks, and if we spent these marks immediately, before the prices of goods had a chance to catch up with the plummeting rate of exchange, we could buy enough food to last us an entire week. The dollar then was truly "mighty," and America was thought of as "the land where the sidewalks are paved with gold." But there was also much ambivalence regarding America. We were told that it was a cultural wasteland, inhabited by people who had no artistic standards. The United States was also supposed to be the prime exponent of capitalism at its worst. And for Bertolt Brecht, who had strong socialist and Marxist leanings, capitalism and decadence were synonymous.

From the musical point of view, America had other attractions. Ragtime, blues, and jazz were swamping Europe. Obviously an American setting would also mean an exploitation of these fashionable new musical idioms. To point up this American side of *Mahagonny*, Brecht did not write any German words for two of its catchiest tunes: "Alabama Song":

and "Benares Song":

They have always been sung in English. When the entire opera is sung in English, as it is in this performance, we cannot appreciate the effect produced in Germany in 1929 by "Moon of Alabama" and the "Benares" tune. These songs gave the German audiences the same special feeling of authenticity that we get when we hear Americans singing Russian operas in Russian.

The American environment of *Mahagonny* is only one side of the story and not its most important side. This opera is also an example of a new form of dramatic presentation, which its creator, Bertolt Brecht, called the "epic" theater, and which, I think, is better described as the "activist" theater. According to Brecht, the audience of the conventional theater is lulled into passive enjoyment, while in the new theater he was promoting, the public would be made to face important issues and would be prodded into intellectual evaluation and personal decision making. "In the old theater of passive enjoyment," he wrote, "a member of the audience would say: 'Yes. This is believable. I remember having also felt that way. I am shattered by the suffering of these characters. Their fate is inescapable.'" In the new "activist" theater, the reaction of the beholder would be quite different. "This is very startling and not to be believed," the spectator would say. "This should not be permitted. The suffering of these characters shatters me because it could be avoided. There *are* alternatives." Brecht wanted the audience to observe, think, and make decisions. It was his avowed purpose to keep the spectators cool, detached, and cynical, watching the characters and actions onstage without passionate subjective identification. Brecht called this new attitude of the audience *Verfremdungseffekt*, which can be translated as a "standing at a distance" or "alienation."

To facilitate this "distancing" effect, Brecht keeps the spectators on the alert by putting his characters through all sorts of startling and unexpected transformations. In the first act, he involves Jimmy Mahoney (pronounced Ma'-ho-ney), the protagonist of the opera, in all sorts of trivial conversations and unfunny jokes—jokes that, in fact, seem almost embarrassingly out of place. For instance, in the sixth scene, the prostitute Jenny Smith asks Jimmy's advice about her hairdo and whether she should or should not put on some underwear; and in the eighth scene, when his friends suggest that Jimmy should catch a fish or pick a banana, he insists that he would much rather cook his hat and eat it. "Something is missing," he keeps repeating. At this point he acts like a sort of harmless bum who is bored and annoyed with the rules and regulations of the city. To the tune of a typical Russian doggerel ditty, he declares his intention to leave Mahagonny and all it stands for. "We all have learnt the rules of right and wrong, and we have watched the moon the whole night long. Now they have closed the bar of Mandalay, and there's no reason left why we should stay" [209].

After his friends persuade him to return to Mahagonny, Jimmy's attitude undergoes a complete transformation. Just when the audience least expects it, he draws his knife, shoots off his gun, and becomes bumptious and dangerously aggressive. At the end of the first act, when it appears that the city of Mahagonny is going to be destroyed by a typhoon, an even greater change comes over Jimmy Mahoney. "We need no roaring hurricanes," he shouts, "and no howling typhoons. For whatever chaos *they* can cause, *we* men will surpass them." He becomes a rabble-rouser, egging on his comrades to indulge in brutalities, and shouting slogans fit for hooligans and muggers: "If you want a thing and you haven't the cash, then grab the cash. If you pass a rich man, hit him on the head and take his money. Just do as you please!" His ravings culminate in a statement of totally outrageous selfishness that is repeated several times in the course of the next two acts: "As you make your bed, you must lie there. Don't expect *me* to care what *you* do. And if someone should kick, then it's *me*, boy. And if someone *gets* kicked, it will be *you!*"

Even after the hurricane passes by, leaving Mahagonny undamaged, this motto remains the governing rule for the inhabitants of the city. But that is just the beginning. In the second act we are introduced to still other standards of behavior. There are to be only four legitimate activities: gluttony, vulgar sex, brutal sports, and immoderate guzzling of whiskey. In the meantime, the fortunes of Jimmy Mahoney undergo a swift deterioration. He backs the losing contender of a boxing match and finds himself completely broke. Neither his best friend nor his girl offers to help him out in his predicament. Eventually, he is taken to court before a corrupt judge and sentenced to be executed for being unable to pay for his drinks.

Nevertheless, in the process of Jimmy's fall from grace, Brecht shows us a very different aspect of his character. Jimmy participates in two nostalgic and tender duets with Jenny, and, during the night that precedes his execution, he is also permitted to sing a very moving aria. These songs show us that no one is safe in Mahagonny, and that even if the perpetrators of brutalities relent and repent, they soon enough become the victims of the system. Thus we see that in this city of nets and spider webs nothing is sacred: neither love, friendship, nor decency; neither sportsmanship, justice, nor religion.

Brecht's play is thus a savage satire on a social order in which people are permitted to do anything as long as they can pay for it. There was of course nothing new in putting the seamy side of modern society onstage. George Bernard Shaw once compared his country's morals to decaying teeth and himself to a dentist. Brecht, however, wants the audience to evaluate available alternatives. For this purpose he uses parallels and parodies. His analogies echo the images used in various utopias of world literature. We are reminded of the Cloud-Cuckoo-land city of Aristophanes' *The Birds*; of the Abbaye Thélème of Rabelais's *Gargantua*; and of the Yahoos of Jonathan Swift's *Gulliver's Travels*. The birds of Cloud-Cuckoo-land wage a war against the Greek gods, just as the people of Mahagonny reject their god in the third act of Weill's opera. Rabelais's motto "Fais ce que voudra" ("Do as you please") is also the slogan of the Mandalay bar in Mahagonny; the difference is that the inhabitants of Rabelais's "city of desire" are completely virtuous, while the customers of the bar of Mandalay are thoroughly vicious. And the selfishness, gluttony, dirty hands, and sexual promiscuousness of Swift's Yahoos have their obvious successors among Mahagonny's men and women. Of course, the distancing effects of Brecht's "activist" theater are not ends in themselves. They are meant to make us aware of social evils and the need to eliminate these evils. Brecht had rather definite ideas on how that should be accomplished. The trouble with his Marxist solutions is that we have since become familiar with other utopias, such as George Orwell's *Animal Farm* and *Nineteen Eighty-four*.

As we turn to the music of *Mahagonny* to see how it fits in with the theatrical ideas of the librettist, we run into difficulties. Opera, almost by definition, belongs in the theater of enjoyment. We certainly are meant to enjoy the voices onstage and the sounds emerging from the pit and to want to identify with the music being sung and played. Alienation, distancing, and activism are not easy to achieve. Even so, it is extraordinary to what extent Kurt Weill's musical procedures manage to parallel Brecht's dramatic ideas. Weill uses a variety of techniques. To begin with, he turns to the so-called cabaret songs, scurrilous ditties that had their origin in the middle of the last century in low-class French dives. The German poet Heinrich Heine heard the cabaret songs in Paris and reported on them as follows: "These coarse chansonettes make cruel fun not only of sex, but of everything and anything that is proper and decent." There is quite a sprinkling of these satirical cabaret songs in *Mahagonny*. "Alabama Song" is the best known of these. Also popular is "As you make your bed you must lie there, and no one will care what you do," which is heard in each act of the opera [210]. Next to cabaret songs, jazz is probably the best medium for mockery and caricature, and much of it in *Mahagonny* is meant to sound brash, loud, and vulgar. Of course, what sounded vulgar fifty years ago seems rather tame nowadays. Lord knows, we are constantly bombarded with much brasher and louder vulgarity.

But the cabaret songs and early forms of American jazz make up less than one-half of the music of *Mahagonny*. Just as Brecht points his finger at Rabelais, Swift, and Aristophanes, so Weill serves up deformed imitations and parodies of musical passages from many well-known European composers. One is constantly reminded of some familiar piece of music, and the effort to place it helps to create a distancing effect, while the surprise of hearing the music parodied produces something akin to alienation. I realize, of course, that what I am describing may be a purely personal reaction and that others may not experience this sensation of near-recognition of seemingly familiar bits of music. Be that as it may, to my ears the hurricane that rages in the second act of *Mahagonny* is accompanied by an orchestral imitation of a Baroque organ concerto {211}, while the lamentations of those who expect to perish in the storm {212} are reminiscent of the figured Chorale of the Armed Men in Mozart's *Magic Flute* {213}. In another example, near the beginning of the second act, in the scene devoted to gluttony, Jacob Schmidt devours two heifers and a young calf. We are regaled by a rather nauseating concoction of slowed-down Romantic tunes; a bit of a well-known song by Mendelssohn:

is followed by snatches of Gustav Mahler:

and by an imitation of a Ländler by Schubert:

After Jacob Schmidt expires from overeating, there is a choral dirge of post-Romantic counterpoint that is certain to give us more musical indigestion. One wonders whether Brecht and Kurt Weill intended to parody the opening lines of Shakespeare's *Twelfth Night*, "If music be the food of love, play on," with "If love of food be turned to music, play on, give us an excess of it, that surfeiting the appetite may sicken and die!"

As far as I know, there is only one place in *Mahagonny* where the composer quotes a tune in its actual, unchanged form. It is in the ninth scene of the first act, where we hear *La Prière d'une vierge* (*The Maiden's Prayer*), by the Polish composer Thekla Badarczewska. She was the most-famous woman composer of her time, and this piano piece, known to everyone in Germany, was generally considered the most atrocious musical trash [214]. The notion of having something entitled *The Maiden's Prayer* played in a bar frequented by prostitutes, is funny enough. But when Jacob Schmidt declares in all seriousness, "That's what I call great art!" the librettist obviously means to heap ridicule on the abysmally low level of musical taste prevalent among the people of Mahagonny. It is a shame that this double joke cannot be adequately appreciated today, when the tune is forgotten and when *A Maiden's Prayer* does not form a part of the feminist repertoire.

In the end, lawlessness, anarchy, and moral decay destroy Mahagonny and all its inhabitants. In the final scene of the opera, as Jimmy's casket is carried onstage, the people sing: "Nothing you can do will help a dead man!"

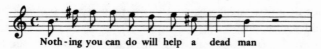

This music reminds me of a passage in Janáček's *Jenůfa*, where young people are advised to "endure their troubles with patience." But Brecht and Weill say "No! Do not endure them. Don't wait until you are dead. Nothing you can do will help a dead man. Don't endure the world, change it" [215].

SALOME

by Richard Strauss

Broadcast March 18, 1972   Cassette illustrations 216–233

THE SUBJECTS OF the opera *Salome* are probably the most extraordinary ever chosen by a composer: an Oriental ruler consumed with lust for his own stepdaughter, who also happens to be his niece; and the maiden, an innocent virgin of sixteen, who develops a compulsive desire for the attentions of a religious ascetic and, when thwarted in her wishes, moves heaven and earth to have the man decapitated so that she can satisfy her longing by kissing the lips of his severed head! No wonder that at its first appearance Strauss's opera was considered perverse, nerve-racking, monstrous, and scandalous.

The music, far from softening this morbid subject, magnifies and underscores every lurid detail, clothing its magnificent depravity with every shimmering hue available on the palette of the modern hundred-piece orchestra. For sheer nervous tension, this work far surpasses anything previously created. The audience is led from horror to horror, while the expectation of impending doom pervades the atmosphere from the moment the curtain opens. Strauss delights in jangling the nerves of the listeners with strident and terrifying dissonances. The next moment he lulls the audience into security with the most mellifluous harmonies, only to strike out again with new tonal clashes.

This mixture of harmonic styles is one of the most fascinating aspects of the score. And it serves to point up the enormous contrast between the inspired prophet, Jokanaan, and the totally unstable and neurotic Herod. In the music that accompanies their first appearances onstage, Jokanaan makes a noble and majestic entrance [216], while Herod staggers almost hysterically onto the terrace of his palace [217].

Nowhere is the contrast between musical loveliness and dissonance more apparent than in the first confrontation between Salome and Jokanaan. As soon as Salome sees Jokanaan she develops a physical longing for him, and she does not hesitate to express it quite brazenly. "I am in love with your body, Jokanaan," she tells him. "Your body is white like the lilies of the field that the mower has never mowed. Your body is white like the snows that lie on the mountains. The white roses in the gardens of the Queen of Arabia are not so white as your body. Let me touch your body, Jokanaan!" Strauss's orchestra depicts this amorous outburst with the most gorgeous splashes of symphonic color [218]. But Jokanaan rejects Salome's advances, and her admiration changes to disgust. "Your body is hideous" she says. "It is like the body of a leper. It is like a plastered wall where vipers have crawled, where scorpions have made their nest!" Here the composer delights in finding the most gruesome dissonances to illustrate the horrible imagery of the leper, the vipers, and the scorpions [219].

Now Salome's desire finds a new outlet. "It is of your hair that I am enamored, Jokanaan" she says [220]. "Your hair is like a cluster of black grapes. The long black nights when the moon hides her face are not so black as your hair. The silence that dwells in the forest is not so black." The instrumental music swirls in a waltzlike undulation to evoke Salome's fascination with the curling black locks of the prophet [221]. A harsh rebuff by Jokanaan leads to a new wave of revulsion on the part of the enamored maiden: "Your hair is horrible. It is covered with mire and dust. It is like a knot of black serpents writhing round your neck." All this Strauss translates into musical horror [222].

And now we are ready for the final and irreversible craving of the girl: "It is your mouth I desire, Jokanaan. The pomegranates that bloom in the garden of Tyre—and are redder than roses—are not as red as your mouth. The red blasts of trumpets that herald the approach of Kings are not so red. Your mouth is redder than the feet of men who tread the wine in the wine press. Your mouth is redder than the feet of the doves that haunt the temples and are fed by the priests." Strauss takes full advantage of this climactic moment of Salome's infatuation and produces a most gorgeous outpouring of symphonic splendor [223]. Quite naturally, he cannot resist the temptation of giving orchestral illustrations of the "blasts of trumpets that herald the approach of Kings":

the tread of the men who stamp on the grapes in the wine press:

and the cooing and twittering of the temple doves:

In the orchestral accompaniment of the final luscious passage, Strauss creates the precise imagery used by Salome in describing the redness of Jokanaan's lips [224].

But these are just details in the overall picture. What is essential is that Salome's longing for Jokanaan's mouth now becomes a compulsive craving. Her monomania is symbolized by the vocal phrase "Ich will deinen Mund küssen, Jokanaan!" which is then repeated over and over again in the orchestra [225]. Salome is hardly aware of what is happening around her. At this point the young Captain of the Guards, Narraboth, who is himself desperately in love with her, can no longer endure listening to these entreaties of love. "Princess, Princess," he begs her, "you, who are like a garden of myrrh, who are like the dove of all doves, do not look at this man. Do not speak such words to him. I cannot bear to hear them!" But Salome pays no attention to him. "I want to kiss your mouth, Jokanaan," she continues to implore, and the phrase mounts higher up the scale.

The tension of the scene now reaches its highest point, as Narraboth, in a desperate attempt to stop Salome, stabs himself and falls between the princess and the prophet [226]. But she does not even notice the death of the man who adored her more than life itself. Ignoring his body completely, she keeps on, like one possessed, with her *idée fixe*, pitching the plea even higher [227].

In creating the morbidly neurotic mood of *Salome*, Strauss is greatly helped by the imaginative text of Oscar Wilde. The symbolic references to such natural phenomena as the moon and the wind are used by the composer to full advantage. The moon, whose brightness illuminates the scene from the first, continuously mirrors the underlying tensions of the drama. The unconscious yearnings and neurotic fears of the characters are symbolically revealed by their attitude toward the moon. Only the prophet Jokanaan, whose spirit dwells in the contemplation of the sunshine of religious truth, is untouched by nocturnal light.

The opening line of the opera is Narraboth's wonderful phrase: "How beautiful is Princess Salome, tonight" [228]. Then the Page remarks that the moon is "like a woman arising from the grave." But the lovesick Captain of the Guard disagrees. For him, the moon is "a little princess whose feet are like white doves. One might imagine she was dancing" [229]. To Salome, fleeing the covetous glances of her stepfather, the moon is "a silver flower, cool and chaste, with the loveliness of a virgin who has remained pure" [230]. The superstitious Herod finds that the moon is like a "crazy drunken woman, reeling through the clouds, looking for lovers" [231]. Only the imperturbable Herodias, steeped in vice and impervious to omens, remains unmoved: "No, the moon is like the moon, that is all."

Near the end, as Salome is lost in the contemplation of Jokanaan's head, the moon disappears behind the clouds, and Herod is seized with terror: "Put out the torches. Hide the moon, hide the stars," he commands the servants. And here, in the dimness of the night we half-witness, half-guess the revolting climax of the action, Salome's kissing of the lips of the dismembered prophet. As the moon comes out again and its beams strike this scene of corruption and horror, Herod gives the final command: "Murder that woman!" The soldiers rush toward the little princess and bury her under their shields.

For the musical realization of this story of Oriental splendor and depravity, Strauss calls upon every musical and instrumental effect which his brilliant craftsmanship and fertile imagination can evoke. Unexpected modulations and scintillating orchestral timbres create effects which, to use his own expression, resemble the shimmer of changing taffeta. Strauss blandly writes passages involving unheard-of difficulties of execution. The orchestral score gives explicit directions for the execution of phrases that at first glance look impossible. Strauss tells the timpani player how to set up his drums so that his two hands can alternate in the playing of a figure the like of which has never before been entrusted to kettledrums:

In another famous passage, the double basses are instructed to squeeze the string tightly between thumb and forefinger while bowing with very short, sharp strokes. The aim is to produce a sound "resembling the suppressed, choked moaning of a woman."

Here and there, Strauss must have felt that his demands exceeded the limit of what could be considered reasonable. In several places, footnotes in the score specify that if a player is unable to execute the notes, they are to be allotted to another instrumentalist or even omitted altogether! No means are considered too grandiose or too cumbersome to achieve a special effect. When, during her contemplation of Jokanaan's head, Salome says: "When I gazed upon you I heard mysterious music," a low A-natural seems to appear from nowhere. The mysterious note actually comes from backstage, where it is played on a pipe organ. A similar effect is used again when Salome finally kisses Jokanaan's lips. Here the organ plays a soft C-sharp minor triad in the low register. This chord is then combined with another clashing chord in the orchestra. The resulting dissonance accompanies and illustrates Salome's words: "Ah, I have kissed your mouth, Jokanaan. There was a bitter taste on your lips. Was it the taste of blood? No, perhaps it tasted of love" [232].

Today, with our musical senses attuned to the idioms which Richard Strauss anticipated and matured with a more objective appreciation for his style, we are no longer scandalized by the story and are able to respond to *Salome* as a work of art. The horrors fall into the background before the surpassing beauty of its musical language. As in any great art work—*Oedipus Rex*, *The Last Judgement*, *Les Fleurs du Mal*—the lurid details are submerged in a flood of magnificence. Art has invested horror with essential beauty, and we surely can paraphrase Narraboth and exclaim with him: "Wie schön ist die Prinzessin Salome heute!" ("How lovely is Princess Salome today") [233].

TANNHÄUSER

by Richard Wagner

Broadcast January 30, 1982   No cassette illustrations

No COMPOSER HAS EVER been as generous in explaining his ideas and intentions as Richard Wagner. His explanations are particularly extensive in regard to his early operas—*The Flying Dutchman* and *Tannhäuser*—the performances of which Wagner could not supervise personally since he was then living in exile in Switzerland and was not permitted to enter Germany. His article *On the Performance of Tannhäuser* is filled with most valuable suggestions concerning musical and dramatic matters and with masterful analytic character sketches of the various roles:

> Tannhäuser's fundamental personality trait is his total immersion in whatever takes place around him. His response is never half-hearted, and being a person driven by powerful instinctive reactions, he is bound to find himself in collision with society. [At the end of the first act] his feeling of repentance is so heartfelt that he shies away from meeting his former companions and rejects their proffered reconciliation. "Let me go," he says. "The path I must follow forbids my return."

Suddenly, says Wagner, this something that can fulfill Tannhäuser's purpose is identified for him by Wolfram's words: "Stay with Elisabeth!"

> Tannhäuser is overwhelmed with joy. "Elisabeth?" Tannhäuser exclaims, "it is a miracle that you mention her adorable name to me!". . . Tannhäuser's past and future flow together with lightning rapidity, like a stream of fire. When he learns of Elisabeth's love for him, the stream melts into the shining lode-star of his new life!

In the same article, Wagner describes in great detail the sequence of events in the opera, with particular attention to Tannhäuser's fluctuating emotional states. Among these thousands of words (for Wagner never said quickly what he could say at great length), there is unfortunately very little mention of the process by which Tannhäuser's beloved Elisabeth is transformed from a young girl, infatuated with a handsome and eloquent minstrel, into the *Heilige Elisabeth*, the wonder-working saint of the last act. There is no doubt that in creating the leading soprano role of the opera, Wagner was inspired by the image of the real Saint Elisabeth, a young woman who lived most of her life in the Wartburg and died in 1231 at the age of 24. Let us see if by assembling some facts and some guesses about the operatic and real-life Elisabeth, we can construct a character sketch of the kind that Wagner provided for the other roles in this opera.

In one of the loveliest Italianate phrases ever penned by Wagner, Wolfram describes the effect that Tannhäuser's songs have had on Elisabeth:

War's Zau - ber, war es rei - ne Macht, durch die solch' Wun-der du voll-bracht,

Wolfram explains that after Tannhäuser left the Wartburg, Elisabeth lost all interest in the tournaments of song; that she stopped attending the celebrations, kept away from the minstrels, and became ill and withdrawn. We are not told why Tannhäuser decided to leave the Wartburg and seek his fortune elsewhere. We can only guess that he saw no prospect of satisfying his sensual desires in the austere atmosphere of the Thuringian court and that he got bored with the insipid love songs of his fellow minstrels. He must also have felt that his love for Elisabeth was hopeless. Wasn't she the Landgrave's niece, a *Fürstin*, a princess, while he was only an ordinary minstrel?

Another question left unanswered by Wagner is, How long did Tannhäuser remain in the Venusberg as guest of the goddess Venus? The medieval legends give us two versions: one legend speaks of one year, another of seven years. I do not like either alternative. Seven years seems excessive, and one year is certainly not long enough. In the second act, the Landgrave is hailed as "Beschützer der holden Kunst" ("protector of the noble art of song"). Even so, it is not likely that more than two song tournaments a year were held in the Wartburg. Let us guess that Elisabeth attended one or two of these after Tannhäuser's departure and then stayed away from the next four or five. On that basis, Tannhäuser remained in the Venusberg for about three years.

Now, then, what was happening to Elisabeth all that time? In the Duet scene near the beginning of the second act, she tells Tannhäuser of the almost hypnotic effect his songs have had on her. They have induced a mixture of sharp pain and sheer delight, alternating with weird feelings and unfamiliar desires. These emotions are expressed most graphically in her music:

Bald wollt' es mich wie Schmerz durch-be-ben, bald drang's in mich wie jä - he Lust,

After Tannhäuser leaves the castle, Elisabeth admits that she has suffered peculiar, painful dreams, while during her waking hours all joy is gone from her heart. This period of alienation and withdrawal lasted a long time, but now Tannhäuser's sudden arrival reawakens Elisabeth's zest for life, a feeling that is so gloriously expressed in the aria "Dich theure Halle grüss ich wieder," Elisabeth's enthusiastic greeting to the Hall of Song, which opens the second act. But Elisabeth is still unsure of herself. In her touching appeal to Tannhäuser she says, "Help me unravel the riddle of my heart, the tangle of my emotional confusion." Oblivious to the hold which the goddess Venus still has on him, Tannhäuser urges Elisabeth to praise the God of Love, who inspired his songs and prompted his return. Then, in a long duet in A-flat major, the enamored pair look forward to future happiness. There is no trace of Elisabeth's saintliness here, only an excited girl in love:

Ge - prie - sen sei die Stun - de, ge - prie - sen sei die Macht,

The change—and what a change!—occurs later in the second act, when Elisabeth is overwhelmed by a blinding realization of her tragic delusion. In fact, there are two separate shocks: first, Elisabeth is stunned into speechlessness by the enormity of Tannhäuser's crime; second, she decides to rush into the fray to protect Tannhäuser from the swords of the outraged menfolk of the Wartburg, who are about to kill him for his brazen flaunting of his sensual delights in the arms of the pagan goddess.

"Haltet ein!" ("Stay away!") Elisabeth exclaims:

She then pleads with the enraged men and begs them to give Tannhäuser a chance to save his eternal soul. I suspect that when setting this moment to music, Wagner was influenced by the almost identical outburst in Beethoven's *Fidelio*, when Leonore confronts the dagger-wielding Pizarro with the cry: "Tödt erst sein Weib!" ("First kill his wife!"):

This climax is the real beginning of Elisabeth's sainthood. Her hopes for personal happiness are now shattered. In the final ensemble of the second act, she addresses heaven, pledging to dedicate herself henceforth only to prayer and repentance. "Take my life, it is no longer mine!"

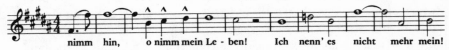

She is even more explicit in her prayerful appeal to the Virgin Mary in the last act: "Whenever I was lured by vain delusions, whenever I was beset by sinful desires and worldly yearnings, I fought against them in a thousandfold struggle so as to kill them in my heart!"

There is a charming legend (set to music by Wagner's father-in-law, Franz Liszt) about one of the minor miracles performed by the real Saint Elisabeth. It seems that she became so generous with her gifts to the poor that she was eventually forbidden to continue her charitable endeavors. One day, when the head of the Wartburg household was returning from hunting, he saw Elisabeth descending from the castle with a heavy bundle filled with bread. He sternly ordered her to open it; she did so, and he saw nothing but a mass of red roses. I like the notion that this sort of thing might have happened to our operatic Elisabeth during the interval between the second and third acts.

This brings up the question of the duration of the pilgrims' march to Rome. These pilgrimages were undertaken, of course, in order to obtain the absolution of sins; and in Tannhäuser they are both musically and dramatically of central importance. The beginning of the Overture and the final chorus both feature one of the main pilgrimage themes:

The motive of remorse and repentance is played by the orchestra and sung by the pilgrims as well as by Tannhäuser:

The song of the younger pilgrims is heard at the end of the second act and then, at the closing of the curtain, Tannhäuser leaves for Rome with them. At the end of the last act, all the pilgrims—young and old—return from Rome.

These pilgrimages to Rome did not take place just any old time, but were carefully planned for the so-called Jubilee Year, the special year when, beginning with Christmas and continuing through all of January, plenary indulgence was obtainable by all the faithful, on condition that they be in Rome, penitently confessing their sins and visiting certain Roman churches. In the second act, Landgrave Hermann refers to this special opportunity of obtaining pardon for one's sins as *Das Gnadenfest* (the Feast of Mercy). Officially the Jubilee Year rituals were instituted by Pope Boniface VIII in the year 1300, but there are indications that informally the Jubilees were observed a few times within each century even earlier than that. There was at one time a special tradition of observing the Jubilees every 33 years (the supposed duration of the earthly life of Jesus). It is therefore not too far-fetched to imagine that there was a Jubilee Year festivity in January 1233. The reason this particular year appeals to me is that it brings the final moments of the operatic Elisabeth very close to the time when the real Saint Elisabeth breathed her last.

In *Tannhäuser* Wagner sidesteps the whole problem of Jubilees and does not mention the exact time of the *Gnadenfest*. The audience is left with the impression that the pilgrims and Tannhäuser leave for Rome in the spring and return in the fall of the same year. To be realistic, I doubt whether in the thirteenth century such a round trip could be completed on foot in four or five months. The distance from the Wartburg (near Eisenach, in the center of Germany) to Rome is about 1,000 miles. Considering the condition of the roads in the Middle Ages and the difficulty of crossing the Swiss Alps, much more than five months would be required for the round trip. I much prefer to believe that the pilgrims and Tannhäuser intended to visit Rome in January and that consequently the time elapsing between the second and third acts would be closer to a year and a half. That gives Elisabeth a more extended period to earn her sainthood; and, if one includes the month of January, the *Gnadenfest* will conform to the tradition and rituals of the Jubilee Years, a point of view which, in my opinion, is indispensable for the full understanding of the opera's dramatic events.

There is one more aspect of *Tannhäuser* that warrants discussion because it has led to much criticism by musicologists as well as by amateurs. What sense does it make, people ask, at the end of the opera, to have the open casket with Elisabeth's body carried down from the castle to the foot of the valley? We know that it was different at first. Wagner tried several solutions before deciding on the final staging. Now, in line with his strict indications, torch-bearing mourners descend from the castle into the valley. The procession is headed by the older pilgrims; then come the minstrels carrying the open casket and finally the Landgrave and the nobility of the countryside. All this, I believe, can be justified easily. The effigy of the Madonna, which is located near the foot of the path, had a special meaning for Elisabeth. In the beginning of the last act, Wolfram remarks that he is certain to find Elisabeth there. Clearly, she came there daily to offer her prayers. It is only logical to assume that, as her dying wish, Elisabeth would request that, immediately after her death, a religious ceremony be held around that particular image of the Virgin Mary. This concept explains the unusual funeral procedure and heightens the impact of the pious hymn sung while the mourners are approaching the sanctuary:

Der See - le Heil, die nun ent-floh'n dem Leib der from-men Dul - de-rin!

It also gives greater significance to the dying Tannhäuser's last words: "Saint Elisabeth, pray for me!"

Hei - li - ge E - li - sa-beth, bit - te für mich!

THAÏS

by Jules Massenet

Broadcast January 28, 1978 **Cassette illustrations 234–247**

T HE STORY OF *Thaïs* deals with a confrontation between the earthly and the heavenly, between sensual and spiritual love. The sensual side is represented by Thaïs, a depraved courtesan of the Egyptian city of Alexandria and a priestess of the goddess Venus; the heavenly love is portrayed by the pious monk Athanaël, who leaves the desert enclave of his Cenobite brothers in order to rescue Thaïs from her life of iniquity. Athanaël is determined to persuade Thaïs to abandon her life of sin and to show her the way to poverty, Christian humility, and virtue. He accomplishes his task: Thaïs gives up the cult of Venus and Eros and takes refuge in the desert nunnery of the saintly Albine. The story has an ironic twist, however. For while Thaïs abandons her pursuit of sinful love, the opposite change takes place in the soul of the formerly chaste Athanaël. The pagan gods take vengeance, and, at the end of the opera, Athanaël is pursued by the demons of carnal desire and sinful lust.

Drastic transformations of this nature are not unusual in opera. The neurotic and frightened Blanche de la Force in *Dialogues of the Carmelites* becomes a saintly martyr, courageously facing death on the guillotine. Total transformations are not uncommon among male operatic characters either. Everyone knows how the loving and generous Otello turns into the murderer of his innocent wife or how—in Bizet's *Carmen*—the law-abiding soldier Don José, becomes a deserter and a murderer. But Massenet's *Thaïs* is the only opera known to me in which *two* transformations—one from depravity to saintliness and the other from piety to lust—occur in the same work.

This tale of extreme contrasts acquires additional dramatic and musical zest from its exotic setting: in the African desert and in the Egyptian city of Alexandria. Toward the end of the last century, opera composers became fascinated with stories that took place in faraway countries: Egypt, India, China, Peru, Palestine, or even relatively nearby Spain. It wasn't only that the stories enabled designers to parade outlandish and colorful settings and costumes; local color could also be injected into the music of the operas by means of unfamiliar bells, drums, and other percussion instruments. The main device, however, for creating exotic musical color lay in the use of unfamiliar scale progressions. Instead of the standard major and minor scales, audiences were regaled with sequences in which various degrees of the scales were raised or lowered.

For instance, instead of the "normal" major scale:

Offenbach in his *Perichole* made this change:

and introduced this tune to highlight the Peruvian element in his charming operetta:

Minor scales lend themselves equally well to exotic deformations in which the second or the seventh degree of the scale is lowered. The priestesses of Dagon in Saint-Saëns' *Samson et Delila* dance to this typically Oriental music:

The Hindu girl in Delibes' *Lakmé* is given this fancy cadenza:

And the Tatar Maiden in Borodin's *Prince Igor* parades this fascinating passage:

Another way of altering a scale is to introduce a skip, known as an "augmented second." Instead of the normal:

we hear the rather shocking:

The complete scale featuring two such skips is sometimes called the "Gypsy" scale:

Bizet used it with great effect to characterize his well-known gypsy heroine, and in *Carmen* we find extended sequences of this scale:

Richard Strauss went one step further and added still another wrinkle to all these exotic refinements. In the beginning of Salome's Dance of the Seven Veils, he combined the augmented interval with the lowered second degree of the scale to produce this highly sophisticated effect:

And I should also like to mention the exotic funeral march during which the unfortunate Persian Prince is led to his death in Puccini's *Turandot*:

There are no gypsies and no funeral marches in *Thaïs*. There is, however, a pervasive Oriental atmosphere and an abundance of lowered seconds and sevenths. The very first theme of the opera establishes the special
mood of the African settlement in the desert by the banks of the Nile by
means of an A-minor scale with the lowered seventh {234}. But Massenet
does not like to rely on just one unusual scale. To create a brilliant pattern
of exotic splendor, he prefers to string together several types of scales. One
colorful example of his Orientalism occurs in the second scene of the first
act, when Thaïs makes her first entrance into the palatial home of Nicias,
a wealthy young man of Alexandria {235}.

Quite apart from their use in creating special exotic effects, harmonies built on altered scales are also of immense help in this opera in setting
off the contrast between Thaïs as a pagan priestess and Thaïs as a convert
to Christianity. To describe her transformation—the process by which she
changes from a pagan courtesan into a repentant and humble daughter of
the Christian church—Massenet constructed the "Meditation," a mar-
velously evocative instrumental interlude, one of the best-known and
best-loved compositions of the French operatic repertoire. In contrast to
the Oriental portions of the score, which are mostly accompanied by
woodwinds and are generously spiced with percussion instruments and exotic scales, this melody is entrusted to a solo violin accompanied by a
harp. It starts out in the purest major mode, untainted by any deviation
from the strict and narrow path of musical virtue {236}. At the opposite
pole of the story, at the end of the drama, the formerly chaste Athanaël
craves to possess the body of Thaïs and is cruelly tormented by the demons
of lust. To create the musical equivalent for this episode, Massenet fashions an orchestral storm that is reminiscent of some of Franz Liszt's wilder
symphonic poems {237}.

So much for the basic dramatic and musical structure of the opera.
The main interest of this work lies in its middle section, in the contest of
wills and persuasive powers of the beautiful and infinitely seductive Thaïs
and the inspired and eloquent Athanaël. At the end of the second act,
Thaïs is the more persuasive one. The passage in which she invites

Athanaël to join the circle of her friends and turn his mind to love ranks with the most cajoling tunes sung by Massenet's seductive heroines [238]. To enhance this melody still further, Massenet embellishes it with an undulating and caressing ornament played by the violins [239]. At this point, Athanaël is merely holding his own. He rejects Thaïs's advances with firmness, but without going into any lengthy explanations.

It is in the first scene of the second act that we witness the real confrontation between these two worthy antagonists. Thaïs not only relies on her own voluptuous charm but also invokes the help of the goddess Venus. She throws some incense into a perfume burner and intones a mysterious incantation, accompanied by Oriental scales and harmonies [240]. In response, Athanaël throws off the rich mantle he was given by Nicias in the preceding scene. Clad only in his tunic, he launches into a mighty oration. Borrowing words from scriptural sources, Athanaël expresses his hope that his voice will sweep forth like the waters of the river Jordan and that his words will melt Thaïs's heart into soft wax [241]. Thaïs seems ready to be convinced, but the voice of her lover Nicias singing offstage, breaks Athanaël's spell. Confused by contradictory emotions, Thaïs imagines that Athanaël—like all the other men she has known—is driven only by selfish motives. Her momentary relapse into her former frame of mind is a necessary dramatic ploy leading to her own sincere transformation, which is illustrated musically by the famous "Meditation."

While Massenet had no trouble finding musical equivalents to portray Thaïs's sinfulness, the visual presentation of her depravity caused him quite a bit of anguish. In his *Souvenirs*, Massenet mentions his attacks of extreme nervousness before the premières of all of his operas. This nervousness was particularly severe before the first performance of *Thaïs*. As usual the composer fled from Paris before the final dress rehearsal. Returning several days after the première, he fully expected to be told that the show had caused a scandal and that he had been disgraced and found guilty of having put onstage "un sujet immoral" ("an indecent subject")! The indecent scenes were of course those in which the scantily clad Thaïs was directed to assume postures, gestures, and gyrations of the goddess Venus. There is no doubt that Massenet was greatly influenced by the Venusberg music of Richard Wagner's *Tannhäuser* and particularly by the Bacchanale danced by the nymphs and satyrs in that opera [242]. As

Thaïs's postures grow more and more striking, so does Massenet's music [243].

To protect himself against the charge of visual immorality, Massenet inserted a special stage direction in the score specifying that during the vision episode of the first scene the half-naked soprano should dance and gesture in such a manner that the audience can see only her back. Unhappily for the composer's peace of mind Thaïs must perform her supposedly lascivious gyrations again at the end of the second scene of the opera. This time Massenet shortened the music of the dance and made certain that the curtain would be rung down long before the threatening striptease had a chance to offend the sensibilities of his audience. We must remember, of course, that the initial performances of this opera took place in the 1890s. We have come a mighty long way since then!

After the stormy events of the second act, the two protagonists are vouchsafed a period of musical and dramatic relaxation. The setting is the oasis where Albine, the head of the saintly retreat of the nuns, will harbor Thaïs until her death. The wells, fountains, and springs of the oasis receive a loving and liquid musical representation [244]; and for the scene in which Athanaël offers the exhausted Thaïs fruit and water, the composer fashions a most charming duet [245].

Massenet is often accused of writing music of excessive sentimentality. This, I believe, is one of those prevalent opinions which are repeated without being examined. It seems to me that the sentiment in Massenet's operas always fits the situation and always develops along perfectly valid dramatic lines. For instance, the melody of the famous "Meditation" [246] does give a glimpse of untroubled bliss. But as the interlude progresses, the music also portrays the concerns, the sorrows, and the repentance through which the sinner must pass before she can be truly worthy of this state of bliss [247].

TOSCA

by Giacomo Puccini

Broadcast April 8, 1978   Cassette illustrations 248–257

THREE SHATTERING CHORDS, played by the combined orchestral instruments *con tutta forza* ("with all their might"), are heard just before the curtain goes up on *Tosca*.

They are heard many times in the opera, but even before we discover with whom or with what this musical sequence is associated, we know that it has to be something extraordinary and utterly frightening. Trying to figure out what produces this powerful effect, one discovers that the progression of the first two chords is actually quite harmless. Had they been followed by a related chord, the entire sequence would sound rather majestic and perhaps would even have some vaguely religious overtones:

It is the third member of the group that creates the sensation of horror. The basses plunge down the wicked interval of the diminished fifth, in parallel motion, which is usually forbidden; and the top note of the second chord leaps up more than two octaves, from E flat to a screaming E natural, forming an interval so outlandish that it does not even have a name. It is as if the knife of a guillotine had suddenly decapitated the first two chords.

The next time this theme appears, its exact meaning is revealed by the words sung by Angelotti: "Scarpia *scellerato!*"

Scellerato is a wonderful Italian word for which we don't seem to have an English equivalent. Basically, it means "villain," but to get the full flavor of *scellerato*, "villain" is not enough. We really have to say "monstrous, fiendish, murderous villain!" Immediately following Angelotti's *scellerato* sentence, Scarpia's theme is heard twice more, this time played very softly by the orchestra, so that Cavaradossi's descriptive words can be heard with utmost clarity:

"Scarpia! That slimy hypocrite whose mask of piety and virtue covers every vice that man can think of!"

Later, when Scarpia himself enters the church, his theme is played again with full force. But this time the wicked third chord is made even more frightening by being prefaced by a violin and flute scale that sounds like the whistle of a whiplash:

For a while the dreaded policeman stands motionless while his inquisitorial glances—always accompanied by the harmonies of his musical theme—dart to every corner of the church:

The Scarpia chords are also heard in a somewhat different context and in an artfully disguised shape. They are preceded by a harmless C-major chord and camouflaged by the intermediate chord of G-flat major, making the strident juxtaposition of A-flat major and E major much less frightening. This new five-chord sequence:

is heard in connection with the hiding place where the fugitive Angelotti will supposedly be safe from Scarpia and his henchmen. In the first act, Cavaradossi, the painter, to the accompaniment of these five chords, tells

Angelotti what to do in case of danger: "If you are desperate, run to the well in the garden. There is water at the bottom, but partway down the well, you'll find a passage that leads to a secret hide-out. In there, you will be safe whatever happens!"

This version of Scarpia's chords occurs again in the second act, during the questioning of Cavaradossi, when the Chief of Police asks Tosca's lover where he has hidden Angelotti. "Again and for the last time, where is he?" The most spectacular episode involving these five chords occurs when Tosca, unable to endure the screams of her tortured lover, reveals to Scarpia the spot where Angelotti is hidden: "In the well—in the garden." "That's where he is hidden?" "Yes!"

As the plot unravels, the full extent of Scarpia's viciousness is revealed. In his brutal police investigations, he does not hesitate to use threats as well as physical and mental torture. Scarpia is also a sadist, a lecher, a blackmailer, a rapist, and a double-crosser! In the first act, when he is planning to use a woman's fan to arouse Tosca's jealousy, he compares himself to Iago, who used a handkerchief to hoodwink Othello. It seems to me that when it comes to total wickedness, Iago cannot hold a candle to Scarpia. Scarpia's behavior is so revolting that everyone is delighted when Tosca stabs the villain and rejoices while watching his death throes, during which his theme also undergoes a subtle transformation. The succession of three chords remains, but the last chord appears in the minor mode, almost as if it had been deprived of its vicious sting:

This funereal, minor-key version of Scarpia's theme is repeated several times before the end of the second act. Even though Scarpia is dead, his spirit lingers on long enough to fulfill his nefarious plotting.

When the last act opens, we see the starlit Roman sky, whose transparency is conveyed in musical terms, as the pre-dawn chill spreads through the scene [248]. It is only when Scarpia's theme is insinuated into this cool atmosphere that we begin to suspect that his vengeance continues [249]. It is Scarpia's ghost that stalks the Roman night! Isn't it extraordinary that with musical themes consisting of a succession of only three or five chords, Puccini is able to produce such far-reaching and profound effects?

Another feat of musical sleight-of-hand occurs at the very end of the first act, where several different melodic lines are superimposed upon just two bass notes—the low F and the low B flat, chimed over and over by the church bells. These melodies, which accompany Scarpia's monologue describing his feelings about Tosca and Cavaradossi, are so different in their expressions of arrogant self-satisfaction, sadistic malice, and lecherous anticipation that it is difficult to believe that they are always accompanied by the same two tones: "Go, Tosca, while Scarpia nestles in your heart." "I will follow wherever love and jealousy guide your footsteps." "Two goals inspire me. First the death of that traitor, then the love of Tosca." "With what rapture I look forward to her embraces!" "Death for her Mario, while Tosca lies safe in my arms!" [250]. At this point, the congregation intones the *Te Deum* hymn, always supported by the same two bass tones: "We praise the Lord" [251]. And then the first act ends, with Scarpia's three chords, the same ones that opened the opera, played triumphantly by the orchestra.

Puccini's sense of economy and his dread of redundancy are almost without parallel in the history of opera. In these days, when we are so impatient with longueurs, when we want to streamline, to condense, to get it over with, Puccini's operas remain as they have always been —untampered with and uncut. Compared with Sardou's play, on which the opera is based, Puccini's *Tosca* is a model of brevity and conciseness. Several characters who play fairly important roles in the original drama do not appear at all in the opera. Tosca's and Cavaradossi's servants have disappeared; and we do not get to see Queen Carolina, or the composer Paisiello, or the Marchese Attavanti (the husband of the lovely lady whose blonde hair and blue eyes were pictured on the painting of Mary Magdalen in the first act).

Instead of Sardou's five acts and six different scenes, the opera has only three scenic pictures. To accomplish this drastic condensation, Puccini and his librettists have done away with the second and third acts of Sardou's drama, which take place in the large ballroom of the Palazzo Farnese and in Cavaradossi's suburban villa. Even so, all the important happenings of the missing sections are revealed, one way or another, in the second act of the opera. Through an open balcony window of Scarpia's apartment we hear the dance music played in the big ballroom by a flute, accompanied by a harp and a viola [252]. This open window also enables us to hear Tosca and the chorus sing the Cantata celebrating Napoleon's presumed defeat in the battle of Marengo [253]. Scarpia closes the window to shut out the sound of Tosca's voice, which interferes with the criminal investigation of Cavaradossi. It is opened again by Tosca, as she threatens to jump to her death rather than permit Scarpia to touch her. Still later, this open window also lets us hear the ominous rat-a-tat of the snare drums presumably accompanying Cavaradossi's march to the gallows:

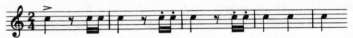

In Puccini's operas there is the most exact matching-up between the thoughts, emotions, and concerns of the characters and the music sung onstage or backstage, or played by instrumentalists no matter where they are located. There are nevertheless a few passages in *Tosca* where, to the puzzlement of commentators and music critics, there seems to be a contradiction between the drama and the music. About four years after *Tosca* was first performed, an American journalist, Arthur Abell, in the course of an interview, pointed out to Puccini that in the second act of the opera, when Floria Tosca is given a choice of either seeing her lover executed or yielding her body to the embraces of the hated Chief of Police, she does not express her anguish and disgust in dramatically and musically appropriate terms, but in an aria set in a major key and featuring the most celestial and melifluous cantilena [254]. "How can Tosca revel in such an outpouring of lyric beauty," Abell asked the composer, "when she knows that the lust-maddened Scarpia is impatiently waiting to rape her?" "You must understand," answered Puccini, "that we Italians have an unquenchable craving for elementary beauty of sound, and that we can express grief, sadness, and mental suffering *most effectively* in a major key. There are situations where pure beauty is preferable to dramatic truth!" Puccini's answer helps to explain another contradiction, which I have always felt at Tosca's very first entrance in the opera, where the same calm and unruffled passage is played by the orchestra. At that point, Tosca is fairly certain that her lover is entertaining another woman, and she is seething with jealousy and anger. Yet the orchestra paints a musical picture of serene and untroubled happiness [255].

In these two instances, I have become fully reconciled to the vocal and orchestral cantilenas, but I cannot help but regret another mismatch, which, in my opinion, weakens the very end of the opera. Tosca's last words, before taking her suicidal leap from the ramparts of the Castle of San Angelo, are "O, Scarpia, avanti a Dio!" They imply that Tosca is ready to appear before the throne of the Almighty and have Him judge her and Scarpia. The thing that troubles me, however, is that the music accompanying her leap is neither her own theme nor that of Scarpia. It is actually the rapturous melody of Cavaradossi's last-act aria, which expresses his delight when welcoming Tosca [256]. Oh, how I wish that instead of apostrophizing the unspeakable *scellerato*, Tosca would address herself to her ideal lover, saying: "O, Mario, Mario, wait for me. I am joining you in Heaven!" And then the gorgeous orchestral outburst at the end of the opera would really make sense [257]!